Here is a book that I can enthusiastically recommend to those who think that we as believers should simply share the gospel and then hunker down and wait for the demise of the United States. This prominent pastor presents the interesting thesis that we cannot prevent the ultimate destruction of our nation, but we can delay it by our involvement in many areas of American life, including politics. Best of all, he is wholly committed to the primacy of the gospel, which ultimately is the only hope for the transformation of the human heart and the restoration of those values on which America was founded. This book is realistic, inspiring, and filled with hope.

—Dr. Erwin W. Lutzer
Senior Pastor, The Moody Church

When Robert Jeffress writes, "The only way to change our nation is by changing the individuals who make up our nation by introducing them to Jesus Christ," he prescribes the only workable and biblical formula that offers hope to this dying land which is now on spiritual, economic, and cultural life support.

—Cal Thomas
Syndicated and *USA Today* columnist, Fox News contributor

Dr. Jeffress is without a doubt a concerned, courageous voice crying out in the wilderness of deception and darkness. What he boldly shares should be prayerfully considered by all who care about our future.

—James Robison
President, LIFE Outreach International

In our current social order, few pastors I have ever known are as courageous or consistent in calling the saints to righteousness as is Dr. Robert Jeffress. *Twilight's Last Gleaming* is a classic case in point, and every believer who reads it will be blessed and stirred to good works.

—Paige Patterson
Southwestern Baptist Theological Seminary

It is an age-old question: Why are we still here? Why is it that, when we surrendered our lives to Christ, He did not immediately take us to be with Him forever? The short answer is this: In the sovereign purposes of God, He intends to accomplish much *in* and *through* His people. In his remarkable new book, *Twilight's Last Gleaming*, Robert Jeffress unpacks and applies this biblical truth in a way that is both insightful and transforming. Surely this is a much-needed book for the church in this hour of human history.

—Frank Wright, PhD
President and CEO, National Religious Broadcasters

# TWILIGHT'S
# LAST
**HOW AMERICA'S
LAST DAYS CAN BE
YOUR BEST DAYS**
# GLEAMING

# ROBERT JEFFRESS

WORTHY
PUBLISHING

Published by Worthy Publishing, a division of Worthy Media, Inc., 134 Franklin Road, Suite 200, Brentwood, Tennessee 37027.

HELPING PEOPLE EXPERIENCE THE HEART OF GOD

eBook available at www.worthypublishing.com

Audio distributed through Oasis Audio; visit www.oasisaudio.com

Library of Congress Control Number: 2011941017

For foreign and subsidiary rights, contact Riggins International Rights Services, Inc.; www.rigginsrights.com

Published in association with Yates & Yates, www.yates2.com

ISBN: 978-1-936034-58-1 (hardcover w/ jacket)

Cover Design: FaceOut Studio
Cover Image: © iStockphoto
Interior Design and Typesetting: Kimberly Sagmiller, Fudge Creative

*Printed in the United States of America*

11 12 13 14 15 16 17 QGFF 8 7 6 5 4 3 2 1

**To Dr. and Mrs. William S. Spears . . .**

*Thank you, Bill and Candye, for your faithful friendship through the years. You are shining examples of what it means to be a light for the gospel of Jesus Christ in this darkening world. I will be eternally grateful for your consistent encouragement to me and to our ministry at First Baptist Church, Dallas.*

# CONTENTS

# FOREWORD

If you are looking for a sweet little "bookette" that is politically correct and safe to read and share with staunch unbelievers so as not to offend them, then put this book down and keep looking.

Dr. Robert Jeffress must not have gotten the memo that says that the pastor of a prominent landmark church that is one of the most influential churches of Christendom is supposed to be noncontroversial, nonconfrontational, and nonpolitical. Uh-oh! This book is bold! Even while maintaining a kind, gracious, and broken spirit, Dr. Jeffress pulls no punches in calling a lethargic church to its feet for the fight to delay a coming collapse of our nation.

Dr. Jeffress made national news when in the fall of 2010, he broke from the ranks of the "bridled" when he openly declared the threat of radical Islam to our country and culture. No politician has been as blunt in describing the enslavement of women, the violence toward dissidents, and the tyrannical rule of those seeking to impose sharia law. And Dr. Jeffress wasn't trying to win votes. In fact, he wasn't even trying to win friends! He was simply proclaiming truth and letting people hear it straight without candy-coating it with preacherisms.

I have admired Dr. Robert Jeffress as pastor of one of the world's great churches and have enjoyed his company and insight as a friend, but in this book, I stand in awe of the clarity of his convictions and the clarion call for believers to come out of hiding and act like they serve a King!

Read this book prayerfully. Then give it to a friend and urge them to read it. Time is of the essence!

Thankfully,
Mike Huckabee

# CHAPTER
# 1

## The Beginning of the End

Several years ago conservative commentator and former Fox News luminary Glenn Beck tapped into the growing sense of angst that Americans—especially Christian Americans—were feeling about the condition of our country. In August 2010, Beck announced he would hold a nonpartisan rally in front of the Lincoln Memorial in Washington D.C. with the goal of "Restoring Honor" to America. Some reports estimated that as many as three hundred thousand people attended the event.

I happened to be in D.C. the day before the rally, so after finishing my meetings I strolled down to the National Mall that warm

Friday evening and was surprised to see hundreds of people already setting up tents along the mall, preparing to spend the night in order to secure a prime spot for the rally. A father who had traveled hundreds of miles with his young family to attend was asked why he had come. "I really don't know, but I realize something is not right in our country and I want to do something about it."

That feeling that "something is not right in our country" is not limited to a group of conservatives crowding the National Mall in Washington. According to a recent Reuters Poll, 73 percent of Americans feel that our country is headed in the wrong direction.[1] I have a feeling that because you picked up this book, you are probably included in that statistic—and for good reason. Perhaps you are deeply disturbed about . . .

- the wholesale effort to remove any and all restrictions on same-sex marriages, abortion, and embryonic stem cell research;
- the failure to protect our borders against illegal immigration, threatening the fiscal and physical well-being of our nation;
- the runaway fiscal deficit that will enslave our children and grandchildren with trillions of dollars of debt;
- the hesitancy of government officials, shackled by political correctness, to recognize and verbalize that we are in a war against terror;
- the willingness to abrogate Americans' First Amendment rights at home to prevent offending Islamic extremists abroad;
- the denial by secularists and even some professing Christians that America was founded as a Christian nation.

You wonder what you should do—and can do—to put the brakes on a country that is seemingly about to go over the cliff. You have an abiding love for your country. You have an even greater allegiance to your Christian faith. You have genuine concerns about the kind of nation in which your children and grandchildren will live.

Whatever his motivation, I admire Glenn Beck for his willingness to do something to help turn around a country that has lost its way. As I left D.C. the Saturday morning of Beck's rally and looked out the airplane window at the hundreds of thousands of patriots gathered below, I began wondering what I could do to make a difference in my country.

## ★ America's Coming Collapse ★

Maybe you, too, are wondering what you can do to help reverse the course of a nation that has lost its way. Well, I have some bad news and some good news for you. The bad news? America's demise is inevitable. I realize that such a statement seems fatalistic, if not downright unpatriotic. Since I first started discussing the concept of this book with friends, I realized just how unpopular such an assertion is. Whenever I described the theme of my book as "How Christians should respond to America's coming collapse," the look on people's faces was akin to that of having been slapped silly: dismay quickly followed by disgust. "America's coming collapse? How could you say such a thing?" I understand why people react that way. Those of us privileged to live in the greatest country in history have been conditioned to believe that the tenacity and resiliency of the American spirit will ultimately triumph over any adversity we encounter. Yet a simple reading of the Bible tells us that America's days are numbered because this planet's days are numbered:

> The world is passing away, and also its lusts; but the one who does the will of God lives forever. (1 John 2:17)

> But the day of the Lord will come like a thief, in which the heavens will pass away with a roar and the elements will be destroyed with intense heat, and the earth and its works will be burned up. (2 Peter 3:10)

> Then I saw a new heaven and a new earth; for the first heaven and the first earth passed away, and there is no longer any sea. (Revelation 21:1)

Notice that American exceptionalism (the idea that America is superior to any other nation that has ever existed) will not exempt our nation from the ultimate destruction that awaits the entire world.

Furthermore, the Bible reveals that America will cease to exist *before* the world comes to an end. According to Daniel 7 and Revelation 17, during the final seven years of earth's history there will be a worldwide dictator (commonly referred to as Antichrist) who will preside over a ten-nation confederacy. All national distinctions will be eliminated, meaning that the United States Constitution will be abolished.

How can I make such an assertion? Our Constitution guarantees our right to elect our governing officials and to worship freely. Yet during the final seven years of history, this worldwide dictator will rise to power without a vote by the American people, and he will abrogate our most cherished freedoms, demanding that he alone be worshipped. Such a usurpation of power can only occur by the abolition of our Constitution. And once the Constitution is gone, the United States of America as we know it will cease to exist.

## ★ Can We Postpone Our Nation's Collapse? ★

Enough of the bad news; here is the good news. Although we can't prevent the ultimate collapse of our nation and destruction of the world, we can postpone it. We have both the ability and responsibility to delay the decay of our nation, even if we can't ultimately reverse it. Why should we work to postpone the inevitable? The same reason we exercise, take medicine, and watch our diets. While those efforts can't prevent our ultimate demise, such actions can delay it!

The motivation for Christians working to delay the coming collapse of our nation is not to preserve our way of life, but to buy more time to share the life-changing gospel of Jesus Christ with as many people as possible before America is swept away by God's judgment.

Most evangelical Christians understand (even if they don't obey) the mandate to serve as lights in this dark world, pointing people to Christ's offer of salvation to all who believe. But I have discovered that many Christians do not comprehend Jesus' command to delay the decay of our culture by acting as salt in the world (Matthew 5:13). Many Christians equate efforts to stop the murder of the unborn, uphold the biblical principles of morality, and elect godly leaders with rearranging the deck chairs on the *Titanic*. "If we are going down anyway, why bother?" people wonder.

I understand that sentiment because I used to feel the same way. During the first eighteen years of my ministry I rarely said anything about social issues from the pulpit and felt no need to encourage my flock to get involved politically. I was not about to sully my pastoral calling by entangling myself in secondary efforts that, according to my understanding of the end times, were futile anyway.

However, I have a different perspective today. While our responsibility to delay our culture's decay is not our primary mission here on earth, it is a necessary prerequisite if we are to fulfill our ultimate calling of pointing people to Jesus Christ. At this critical time in our nation's history, we cannot afford to sit back with folded hands as we wait for the end. God is calling you and me to stand up and push back against the tide of unrighteousness that threatens to engulf our country.

What specifically can you do to effect real change in our country? And how do you balance your primary calling to share the gospel with the calling to stand up against ungodliness in our nation? My trip to Washington D.C. that hot August weekend was the beginning of my own journey to discover the answer to those critical questions that would change my life and ministry forever.

## ★ The Islamic Explosion ★

It was during this same period of time that an Islamic imam in New York City proposed building a mosque near Ground Zero. I had participated in a debate a few weeks earlier on MSNBC with a Jewish rabbi who surprisingly supported building the mosque. I countered that it was no more appropriate for American Muslims to build a mosque at Ground Zero than it would be for Japanese Americans to build a shrine to Emperor Hirohito at Pearl Harbor. Fortunately, television anchor Contessa Brewer unwittingly pitched me a question right over home plate when she asked, "Pastor Jeffress, why are you characterizing Islam with such a broad brush as a violent religion?"

I responded, "Well, Contessa, I have just been listening to your broadcast for the past ten minutes and heard you report about ten Christian relief workers murdered by Muslim gunmen in Afghanistan, then you reported about a Saudi Arabian woman stoned to death for adultery while her lover was set free, and finally you just reported about a German mosque being shut down because it was a launching pad for attacks. The American people are waking up to the true nature of Islam."

With that media confrontation still fresh in my mind, it seemed only natural to say something to my congregation about the debate raging in the country at that time about the mosque at Ground Zero in particular, but also the larger issue concerning Islam itself. After all, a Pew Research poll reveals that 57 percent of evangelical Christians believe that there are multiple paths to God.[2] If Islam is one of those alternate roads that leads to the same God, why should Christians condemn the faith choice of 1.3 billion people on our planet?

Endless conservative commentators argued against building the mosque at Ground Zero, but in the next breath they affirmed, "Islam is a religion of peace." That made no sense to me. If Islam were truly a peaceful religion, then why should anyone object to building a mosque at Ground Zero? If people wrongly associated the religion of Islam with the attacks of 9/11, should we give credence to peoples' distorted view of Islam by refusing to build a place of worship for this so-called religion of peace?

I thought our church's annual "Ask the Pastor" service, during which members ask me any question they desire, would be the perfect forum for me to address the subject of Islam. Maybe this was the arena in which I could stand for truth and contribute in some way to reversing the downward spiral of our nation. No, it wasn't the National Mall, and I wasn't Glenn Beck. But we all have to start somewhere.

That evening a college student asked me to talk about the true nature of Islam in light of recent events. I responded:

It makes no sense for people to say Islam is a peaceful religion and then object to building a mosque at Ground Zero. The truth is that Islam is a religion that incites violence around the world. It is a religion that promotes pedophilia. The founder of Islam—this so-called prophet Mohammed—raped a nine-year-old girl, Aisha, and took her as his bride. Today, Muslim men around the world use his example as an excuse for taking brides—some as young as four years old. It is a religion that oppresses women. Just look at the example of women living under sharia law around the world. But for Christians, the worst thing about Islam is that it is a false religion that leads people away from the true God. As Christians and conservatives it is time for us to take the gloves off and tell the truth about this evil, evil religion.

The congregation immediately rose to their feet in an explosive and sustained ovation. I had taken a stand, said what I thought needed to be said, and was ready to move on to the next question.

Several days later, someone in our church who monitors blogs mentioned to me that a local online publication had picked up my comments on Islam and was posting particularly angry responses from readers. I thought nothing about it until a local television reporter called and asked for a comment from me to run in a less-than-flattering story they were doing about my remarks.

Then a popular columnist (and fellow Baptist) from the *Dallas Morning News* called me for a friendly chat, giving me a chance to either retract or support the statements I had made about Islam. I sent him some sources for my comments, including one from CBS

News relating to the underage marriages in third-world countries that were motivated by Islamic beliefs. His e-mail to me the next day closed with, "Robert, I am afraid you are not going to like my column on Sunday." I did not know how right he was.

## ★ Un-American and Un-Christian? ★

On Sunday morning I, along with many in my congregation, opened the *Dallas Morning News* to find this headline: "Dallas pastor's broadbrush criticism of Islam goes way too far," followed by this opening paragraph:

> It's hard to know where to start in expressing dismay with the Rev. Robert Jeffress—for being uninformed, un-Christian or un-American. The pastor of Dallas' First Baptist Church managed to squeeze all three into a recent rant against Islam. . . .[3]

What followed was a passionate attempt to show that there is absolutely no evidence to support the claim that Islam incites violence around the world, oppresses women, or in any way supports marriage to underage children. The columnist interviewed a theology professor and expert in Islam at a local university who did not deny Muhammad's marriage to a nine-year-old girl but excused it on the basis that the girl "was chosen by God" and became a "trusted source of sayings from Muhammad."[4] Furthermore, the professor said that I was endangering our troops abroad by speaking out against Islam—a claim I found somewhat laughable. Will our enemies hate us less if we say nice things about their religion?

And apparently I was being un-Christian by calling Islam an evil religion. The professor opined that I had broken at least three biblical commandments in my comments, including "Do unto others as you would have them do unto you." The professor must think that Jesus was also un-Christian when He criticized the Pharisees, whom He referred to as a "brood of vipers" (Matthew 23:33).

Knowing that many in my congregation were reading this indictment of their pastor before they came to church, I felt like I had to make a response to the columnist. Before I began my sermon that Sunday, I said that I had a few comments I wanted to make: "Many of you read the column in the *Dallas Morning News* accusing me of being uninformed, un-American, and un-Christian. Whether I am un-Christian and un-American is something readers will have to decide for themselves. But uninformed I am not."

I then delivered a ten-minute rebuttal to the columnist, citing evidence for the claims I had made, and concluded, "And so I stand by my statements from two weeks ago about Islam. It is a false religion, based on a false book, written by a false prophet."

Again, the congregation stood in unison and applauded wildly. Assuming this would end up on the evening news, I felt obliged to add, "For those of you watching on television, please do not equate this applause with a hatred for Muslims. We love Muslims and want to see them come to faith in Jesus Christ. But you can never point people to the right path to God unless you first of all convince them that they are on the wrong path to God."

The statement not only made the evening news, but nearly three hundred thousand people downloaded the video clip from YouTube over the next few weeks, and the church was flooded with e-mails from around the world. The majority were very supportive. Some from Canada and Europe said that I did not present half of what I could have shared about radical Islamists and their goal of world domination. Of course, there were a few who accused me of being demon-possessed or paid by Fox News to make my comments.

But what astounded me was the number of professing Christians who were convinced that speaking out against another religion was inconsistent with the teachings of Jesus Christ. One wrote:

> The [First Baptist Church pastor's] comments about Islam serve only to foster bigotry and hatred, not understanding and tolerance. Anyone who thinks Islam is an evil religion does not understand what Islam is all about, and I am speaking as a lifelong Christian and a Baptist. As for his comments about Islam being a "false religion built upon a false book written by a false prophet"—so what? . . . Being an American and living in the USA means that we tolerate all religions and respect freedom of choice in religious matters.[5]

## ★ The Real Dilemma ★

Even some of my closest friends who agreed with everything I said questioned the wisdom of being so vocal about a potentially volatile subject. Some law enforcement officials warned me of the necessity of increased security around my family and the church. After all, Islamic death warrants had been issued for people making much less inflammatory statements than I had made. Was it really worth endangering my own safety as well as the safety of our congregation by making such incendiary comments?

Our church was just beginning a $123 million building project for our new campus in the heart of downtown Dallas. One trusted deacon who agreed with my comments warned me, "Your comments might jeopardize the church's ability to obtain financing for this project. Do you really want to risk your life, your ability to preach the gospel, and everything you have dreamed of for our church by speaking out against Islam?"

It's one thing to have bloggers criticize your message, methods, and motives. But to hear a friend voice such a concern would make anyone stop and think. It certainly did me. Why did I feel so compelled to speak out against Islam at this particular time? Was I simply capitalizing on the feelings of Islamophobia sweeping the country as America approached another anniversary of September 11? Was the issue really worth endangering my life and jeopardizing my ministry? My brother, who serves as an elder in a Presbyterian church, bluntly asked me, "Would you rather be known as a culture warrior or a preacher of the gospel? If you are not careful, your legacy is going to be the former rather than the latter."

Ouch. During my thirty-five years of ministry I have taken well-publicized stands against homosexuality, abortion, and discrimination against Christians. I have been threatened with physical violence and with the loss of our church's tax-exempt status by the ACLU and other like-minded groups. As America continues to "slouch toward Gomorrah," as Judge Robert Bork described,[6] it is easy to see political and social activism as the quick fix to our culture's social and spiritual ills. Many people think that if we can just elect the right candidates, who in turn will enact the right laws, we can save America. Perhaps you, too, have been tempted to focus on political solutions to reverse the decay that is eroding the moral and spiritual foundation of our nation.

Yet consider the example of the apostle Paul. This warrior for the Christian faith lived under one of the most godless, oppressive regimes in human history. No government was more hostile toward

Christianity than the Roman Empire. In fact, it was Rome's anti-Christian sentiment that was responsible for Paul's imprisonment and eventual martyrdom.

But what was Paul's attitude about his persecution? Did he pen a letter from prison with the underlying theme "when bad things happen to good Christians like me"? Did he attempt to mobilize Christians into a political movement that would overthrow the Roman emperor Nero? To the contrary, Paul was amazingly sanguine about his imprisonment. Nineteen times in his short letter to the Philippians Paul refers to *joy*, *rejoicing*, or *gladness*. Why was Paul so upbeat about his depressing situation? He explains in his opening words:

> Now I want you to know, brethren, that my circumstances have turned out for the greater progress of the gospel, so that my imprisonment in the cause of Christ has become well known throughout the whole praetorian guard and to everyone else, and that most of the brethren, trusting in the Lord because of my imprisonment, have far more courage to speak the word of God without fear. (Philippians 1:12–14)

Had Paul's goal in life been an existence filled with pleasure and void of pain, then his imprisonment would have been a tragedy. He would have written, "Now I want you to know, brethren, that my circumstances have turned out to be a giant detour in my plan for my life." But Paul had a greater purpose for living than peace and prosperity. He had dedicated his life to sharing the good news of Jesus Christ with as many people as possible. And it was through the lens of that grand purpose that he viewed every circumstance in his life, including his suffering.

The result? Far from being a catastrophe, Paul's imprisonment served as a catalyst in helping him fulfill his mission. Because Paul was in chains, other Christians were being emboldened to share their faith like the apostle. Paul's focus was not on reversing the social injustices that had landed him in jail but on the great opportunity these injustices had provided him to share the good news of Jesus Christ. But the apostle doesn't stop there.

## ★ Against the Night ★

Paul moves beyond his own situation, encouraging you and me to adopt the same purpose and therefore utilize the same lens through which to view the dark culture in which we live:

> Do all things without grumbling or disputing; so that you will prove yourselves to be blameless and innocent, children of God above reproach in the midst of a crooked and perverse generation, among whom you appear as lights in the world, holding fast the word of life, so that in the day of Christ I will have reason to glory because I did not run in vain nor toil in vain. (Philippians 2:14–16)

I want you to carefully reread the phrase "in the midst of a crooked and perverse generation." Is there any better description of the culture in which we are living, more than two thousand years later? Someone has said that there is no century more like the first century than the twenty-first century. Both are characterized by wholesale immorality and hostility toward Christianity.

Yet Paul did not admonish the Christians in Philippi to straighten out their crooked culture. He did not call on them to instigate a rebellion against the Roman government. Instead, he reminded them that against the darkness of their world they were to be "children of God . . . holding fast the word of life."

Several weeks ago I gained a little more insight into the metaphor Paul is employing in this passage. My youngest daughter was getting ready to leave for her freshman year in college, so I invited her to go shopping with me, thinking we would spend an hour or so at the mall, perhaps purchasing a dress from her favorite store.

But as soon as we arrived at the shopping center, she made a beeline into a jewelry store. She already had in mind what her parting gift would be, and it would cost more than I had anticipated spending! She had her heart set on a ring she had seen a few weeks earlier and asked the salesman to see it again.

I knew immediately this jeweler was an experienced salesman. Instead of simply bringing us the ring to inspect, he first laid a piece of black felt on top of the display counter. He then placed the ring on top of that black cloth. The brilliance of the ring nearly blinded me—even to the price. It was spectacular! The salesman understood a truth about jewelry that the apostle Paul understood about the gospel message: the darker the background, the brighter the light.

The jeweler had one purpose in his encounter with us: to make the sale. Instead of cursing the black felt background, the jeweler used the darkness to highlight the beauty of the stone, creating in us an even greater desire to purchase the ring.

The apostle Paul was also motivated by a singular purpose in life: "selling" the gospel of Jesus Christ to as many people as possible. Assuming that the Philippians, as well as all of us who are Christ-followers, would be inspired by the same purpose, Paul encourages us to take advantage of the darkness of the culture in order to highlight the brilliance of the Light of the World, Jesus Christ. We are to appear in this dark world "as lights . . . holding fast the word of life." (Philippians 2:15-16).

Instead of allowing the daily flow of negativity from the media or forwarded e-mails from friends to drive us to despair, we should see our present situation for what it is: an unprecedented chance to point people to the hope of Jesus Christ. Why? The darker the background, the brighter the light!

## ★ What Is Your Focus in Life? ★

I'm convinced that one reason Christians are so discouraged and frightened about the condition of our country is that, unlike the apostle Paul, their lives are focused on personal peace, prosperity, and the avoidance of pain. No wonder they are frightened by terrorist threats, health-care reform, fiscal insolvency, and open hostility to all things Christian. They realize that their private worlds are in danger of being turned upside down. After all, if the focus of your life is money, then the thought of higher taxes is very disturbing. If the focus of your life is convenience, then the prospect of government-run health care is a nightmare. If the focus of your life is avoiding death, then the prospect of a terrorist attack is alarming.

Recently in a sermon I encouraged our members to watch cable news less and read their Bibles more to gain God's perspective on the world. I mentioned one specific commentator whose daily homilies would cause anyone to want to retreat into an underground bunker while awaiting the end. Boy, did I hit a nerve! One elderly couple in our church confronted me and said, "We can't believe you told us to quit watching that commentator. We *have* to watch him every day because we're old, and we're afraid!" As my children used to say to me, "Thank you, Captain Obvious." No wonder this couple is fearful!

But the real answer to this couple's fear is not just a change of channels but a change of focus. Fear is like a warning light on the dashboard of your car. When the Check Engine light appears, you probably don't drive to the dealer and say, "I've got a problem with my car. This warning indicator won't go off. Would you please disconnect the light?" The illuminated light is an indicator of something else wrong with your car.

In the same way, fear is not so much a problem itself as an indicator of something else wrong in your life. Almost without exception anxiety is an indicator that we have built our lives around the temporal rather than the eternal. When our sense of well-being in life depends on our net worth, our jobs, our health, or our family, then we become fearful when those things are threatened.

But when we share the same passion that permeated every fiber in Paul's life—the spreading of the kingdom of God throughout the world—then we will view a darkening and threatening world differently. Government instability, economic uncertainty, cultural decay, and international chaos provide the perfect backdrop for displaying the contrasting brilliance of Jesus Christ. Instead of cursing the darkness, we should welcome it!

When Paul encourages Christians to appear as lights in the world, he is simply echoing the words of Jesus Christ:

You are the light of the world. A city set on a hill cannot be hidden; nor does anyone light a lamp and put it under a basket, but on the lampstand, and it gives light to all who are in the house. Let your light shine before men in such a way that they may see your good works, and glorify your Father who is in heaven. (Matthew 5:14–16)

Imagine walking into your home one night after having dinner out with your spouse. What is the first thing you do when you walk into a dark house? Do you start whining, "Why, oh why, is it so dark in here? I'm afraid of who might be lurking in the corner, ready to pounce on me"? Or would you say to your spouse, "I don't care for this darkness. We need to sell this house and move to someplace where there is more light"? Instead of complaining about or fleeing from the darkness, you would simply displace the darkness by turning on the light! The best remedy for darkness is light.

Jesus is reminding all of His followers that He has left us in this world for a reason. We are here not to fear the darkness or abandon the darkness, but our assignment is to displace the darkness by holding up the light of the gospel. Jesus, the Light of the World, has returned to heaven. But while He is away preparing for His return to earth, He has installed an auxiliary lighting system in the world. It is called the church. In the book of the Revelation, the apostle John compares the church to seven golden lampstands, illuminating the Lord Jesus Christ (Revelation 1:12, 20).

## ★ Left Behind . . . for a Reason ★

All of this talk about Christians being the light of the world is not just some warm, devotional thought to encourage you to be nicer to other people. You will never understand your purpose for living until you grasp this concept. If you ask the average Christian, "What do you think God's purpose for your life is?" they will hem and haw, or give you a deer-caught-in-the-headlights stare.

Ask a more mature Christian the same question about his purpose in life and he might answer, "To enjoy fellowship with God." That sounds like a good response, until you think about it. If God's purpose for your life was to enjoy a relationship with Him, then it only makes sense that the moment He saved you, He would zap you off this planet and take you to heaven, where you could enjoy a perfect relationship with Him. Frankly, God could enjoy a much more fulfilling relationship with you in heaven than He is experiencing with you on earth.

After all, God is lucky to get a few minutes alone with most of us each day. He continually has to compete with distractions for our affection and attention. No wonder the famed evangelist of yesteryear Billy Sunday used to say that the best thing a person could do would be to come to one of his revivals, get saved, walk out into the street, get hit by a truck, and go immediately to heaven! There, the new convert could enjoy a perfect relationship with God for eternity, untainted by sin.

But Jesus and Paul are saying God's plan for our lives is different than Billy Sunday's "get saved, get killed, go to heaven" plan. God has chosen to temporarily forgo a better relationship with you in heaven and leave you in this dark world for one purpose: to light up the place with the good news of Jesus Christ!

You are not here to build a bulging portfolio of financial assets, to make a name for yourself, or to wring as much pleasure as possible out of the seventy or eighty years of your life. Instead, God chose to leave you on earth to point as many people as possible to the saving power of Jesus Christ. The Lord was clear about His reason for coming to earth: "The Son of Man has come to seek and to save that which was lost" (Luke 19:10). And Jesus was equally clear about His reason for leaving you and me on the earth. His final command to His disciples was, "Go therefore and make disciples of all the nations" (Matthew 28:19).

Without trying to put you on a guilt trip, let me ask you a simple question. What is your strategy for fulfilling Jesus' command? You probably have some kind of plan to earn a degree from school, to further your career, to help your children maximize their potential, and to provide for your family's current and future financial needs. What is your plan for fulfilling the one purpose for which God has left you on earth?

If you don't have such a plan, you are not alone. A few months ago when I started focusing on the unique calling of Christians to be lights in this crooked and perverse generation, I challenged our church members who were sincerely concerned about the direction of their nation to join me in the only strategy that will make a lasting difference in our country. Face it, both the Republican and Democratic political parties are ideologically bankrupt when it comes to reversing the downward course of our country. The only way to change our nation is by changing the individuals who make up our nation by introducing them to Jesus Christ. With the rallying cry "The only way to save America is by saving Americans," one thousand of our congregation's members committed to becoming part of what we called The Pastor's Light Force—a group of men and women who wanted to change our nation by introducing people to Jesus Christ.

Realizing that most Christians don't have a strategy for being lights in the world, we shared with these thousand members a simple strategy for introducing people to Jesus Christ—a strategy I will describe in chapter 5.

## ★ Don't Forget to Add Salt ★

Am I insinuating that Christians are to make evangelism their sole focus in life and withdraw from any political involvement? Not at all. Jesus said that Christians have another role in this world besides serving as light.

> You are the salt of the earth; but if the salt has become tasteless, how can it be made salty again? It is no longer good for anything, except to be thrown out and trampled under foot by men. (Matthew 5:13)

In the days before refrigerators, salt was used to keep meat from spoiling. Salt prevented premature decay. However, eventually the meat would decay and have to be discarded. Salt couldn't prevent decay; it could only give meat a longer shelf life.

When Jesus encourages believers to be salt in the world, He is reminding us that while we will never be able to reverse the decay in our culture caused by the curse of sin, we can slow down the process. By how we live and what we do, we can delay the collapse of our nation and our world. In describing the final world ruler, commonly referred to as the Antichrist, the apostle Paul writes:

> And you know what restrains him now, so that in his time he will be revealed. For the mystery of lawlessness is already at work; only he who now restrains will do so until he is taken out of the way. (2 Thessalonians 2:6–7)

Specifically, Paul refers to the church as the force that is restraining the torrent of evil that will finally be poured out during the final seven years of earth's history. Perhaps this visual image will help you understand the truth Paul is teaching.

Picture fifty thousand Christians with their backs pressed against Hoover Dam as leaks begin springing out from the loosened bricks in that massive structure. This band of believers realize they will not be able to prevent the eventual collapse of the dam, but perhaps they can postpone it for a little while so that as many residents as possible who are living in the path of the inevitable flood can be saved. Their goal is not to repair the dam but to stall the collapse of the dam in order to rescue people.

Similarly, there is nothing you and I can do to prevent the eventual collapse of the world under the weight of sin—a collapse that will coincide with God's final judgments during the Tribulation and the return of Jesus Christ. It is all part of God's immutable plan. The role the United States of America will play during those final years of earth's history is unclear. What is clear is that our nation will not be exempt from God's final judgment against the earth, indicating that we will not be able to reverse the downward spiral of sin. But we can postpone it.

Delay God's judgment? You may be wondering, *Don't you believe in the sovereignty of God? Don't you realize that there is nothing we can do to postpone the day of judgment that God has already placed on His calendar?* After two advanced seminary degrees and thirty-five years of preaching and teaching the Bible, I must confess that God's sovereignty is a mystery I cannot begin to fathom. But what is clear to me from Scripture is that our action—as well as our inaction— does have real consequences.

Consider the prophet Jonah's activities in the wicked city of Nineveh, the capital of Assyria. Through the preaching of this reluctant prophet, many of the city's residents repented of their evil wickedness. And how did God respond?

When God saw their deeds, that they turned from their wicked way, then God relented concerning the calamity which He had declared He would bring upon them. And He did not do it. (Jonah 3:10)

I have read and heard countless attempts to explain away this verse. "What this verse *really* means is that . . ." Here's a good rule of thumb for interpreting the Bible: when the plain sense makes good sense, seek no other sense! The text plainly says that God had planned to rain down judgment upon the residents of Nineveh. However, because they turned away from sin, God postponed His destruction of the city, which eventually did collapse in 612 BC. What was the catalyst for the Ninevites' change of heart that led to God's change of mind? The actions of one man named Jonah.

## ★ You Can Make a Difference ★

Although this story raises as many questions as it provides answers, one principle flashes like a neon sign: believers *can* make a difference in their world. From our admittedly limited perspective, we can postpone God's judgment against our nation by acting as salt and preserving righteousness in our nation.

Why should we care about delaying the inevitable judgment of God? For one reason: to give unbelievers a little longer to turn to Jesus Christ and escape eternal separation from God. People frequently ask, "Why does God allow evil to run rampant in the world? Why doesn't He just go ahead and send Christ back to reclaim the world and end this whole mess?"

The apostle Peter answered that question in his final letter to a hurting church. Christians who were enduring tremendous persecution were asking the apostle, "Why doesn't Christ return and end our suffering?" Unbelievers were asking a variation of the same question: "If Christ really exists, why doesn't He come back and fulfill His promise?" Peter says there is only one reason that God is allowing the world to continue as it is before He draws everything to a close:

> The Lord is not slow about His promise, as some count slowness, but is patient toward you, not wishing for any to perish but for all to come to repentance. But the day of the Lord will come like a thief, in which the heavens will pass away with a roar and the elements will be destroyed with intense heat, and the earth and its works will be burned up. (2 Peter 3:9–10)

Here is a revealing glimpse into the heart of God. Yes, He is a God of judgment, but He is also a God of mercy. His desire is not to judge as many people as possible but to save as many people as possible. One mark of a true follower of Christ is that we mirror that same passion for rescuing those who are in danger of being swept away by the flood of God's final judgments.

Joni Eareckson Tada has spent more than forty years in a wheelchair as a quadriplegic. Recently, she was also diagnosed with breast cancer. An interviewer asked Joni the inevitable question: "Why does God allow suffering in the world instead of ending it all with His return?" Joni answered, not as an armchair theologian but as a wheelchair-bound disciple who reflects the redemptive heart of God:

> The rule of thumb is that we experience much suffering because we live in a fallen world, and it is groaning under the weight of a heavy curse. If God being good means he has to get rid of sin, it means he would have to get rid of sinners. God is a God of great generosity and great mercy, so he is keeping the execution

of suffering. He's not closing the curtain on suffering until there is more time to gather more people into the fold of Christ's fellowship.[7]

Joni correctly reasons that an end to her suffering would also mean an end to unbelievers' opportunity to trust in Christ. So she waits patiently for that future day while she works to be salt and light in the present day. If Joni is willing to stay in her wheelchair a little longer and postpone her eventual healing so that others might come to know Christ, shouldn't we be willing to get up out of our chairs and do whatever we can to delay the inevitable "closing of the curtain" for the same purpose?

## ★ Standing Up and Shining Bright ★

This book is about what you and I can do during these final years of earth's history—or of our own history—to be the salt and light Christ commanded us to be. Notice that Jesus' instruction to be salt and light (Matthew 5:13–15) is not an either/or command but rather, a both/and mandate. As light, we are to illuminate the saving power of Jesus Christ. As salt, we are to stand up against the tide of unrighteousness that is sweeping our country, evidenced by the wholesale acceptance of sexual perversion, cruelty toward children, and idolatry. As we will see, these are three sins that are guaranteed to bring God's judgment against any nation.

Unfortunately, many Christians have adopted an attitude of passivity toward those sins God has labeled as abominations: homosexuality, the murder of unborn children, and elevation of false gods at the expense of worshipping the true God. We have cloaked our indifference with piety ("I'm going to focus on my relationship with God"), theology ("I can't change God's sovereign plan"), and even patriotism ("I shouldn't impose my morality on others in a free country").

Yet whenever God's people refuse to be salt and stand up against unrighteousness, evil always triumphs. And God's judgment always comes. We only have to travel back in history sixty-five years to see the end result of passivity that is covered in a veneer of piety, theology, and misplaced patriotism. Many German Christians used all three rationales for excusing their inaction against the evil of Adolph Hitler.

Erwin Lutzer recounts a testimony from a Christian living in Germany about the end result of indifference:

I lived in Germany during the Nazi Holocaust. I considered myself a Christian. We heard stories of what was happening to the Jews, but we tried to distance ourselves from it, because, what could anyone do to stop it? A railroad track ran behind our small church and each Sunday morning we could hear the whistle in the distance and then the wheels coming over the tracks. We became disturbed when we heard the cries coming from the train as it passed by. We realized that it was carrying Jews like cattle in the cars! Week after week the whistle would blow. We dreaded to hear the sound of those wheels because we knew that we would hear the cries of the Jews en route to a death camp. Their screams tormented us. We knew the time the train was coming and when we heard the whistle blow we began singing hymns. By the time the train came past our church we were singing at the top of our voices. If we heard the screams, we sang more loudly and soon we heard them no more. Years have passed and no one talks about it anymore. But I still hear that train whistle in my sleep. God forgive me; forgive all of us who called ourselves Christians yet did nothing to intervene.[8]

It's time for Christians to intervene. In the chapters that follow we will discuss some practical ways to stand up against the rising tide of evil that is destroying our nation. In our discussion we will tackle some difficult dilemmas such as . . .

- Should Christians join with Mormons and other non-Christian groups to oppose abortion and same-sex marriages?
- Is it better to elect a qualified non-Christian or an unqualified Christian to office?
- Should Christians seek preferential treatment for their faith in a pluralistic society?
- What would Jesus really say about health-care reform, fiscal policy, and illegal immigration?
- When should Christians disobey the government?

## ★ Don't Forget the Mission ★

We must never lose sight of our ultimate goal in standing up against unrighteousness. God has not called us to save our country. Instead, He has commanded us to save those who are living in our country from His coming judgment. Salt restores nothing; it only buys us a little more time to shine the light of the gospel in this increasingly dark world.

Allow me to be blunt. Outlawing same-sex marriages, reducing the number of abortions performed each year, or displaying the Ten

Commandments in every classroom in America will not increase the eventual population of heaven by one solitary person apart from the proclamation of the gospel. In fact, if we are not careful, we could actually decrease the number of people in heaven if we ever compromise our long-range mission to achieve short-term goals.

When a prominent Christian leader joins with a popular member of a non-Christian cult to fight immorality and justifies the alliance by saying, "We have to save America first and then worry about theology," he is telegraphing the not-so-subtle message that temporal concerns supersede eternal issues.

Most people have been conditioned to relegate theology to irrelevant issues like the number of angels dancing on the head of a pin or speculative topics such as predestination and free will. However, *theology* is "the study of God." What could be more important than a person's understanding of his Creator and what He requires of His creatures? As A. W. Tozer wrote, "What comes into our minds when we think about God is the most important thing about us."[9] A person's belief about God shapes his life on earth and determines his destiny for eternity. When Christian leaders imply that the differences between Christianity and a cult like Mormonism are minimal compared to their agreement on social concerns, we are in danger of jeopardizing our unique mission to be lights in this dark world.

I was recently invited to lead a pro-life march of several thousand people in Dallas to the Dallas city courthouse, where the landmark case *Roe v. Wade*, legalizing abortion in America, began. The march was to begin in front of another church that denies that faith in Christ alone is the only way to be saved. By joining hands with the leader of that church and marching together to protest abortion, what message would I be communicating? Is it possible that someone seeing me alongside this religious leader might assume that the differences in our beliefs are inconsequential? Could my actions cause someone to become part of that congregation and embrace a belief system that will result in his eternal separation from God? Would I have not only surrendered but actually sabotaged my most important calling as a Christian in order to achieve a lesser goal? Honestly, I'm still wrestling with those issues.

However, I'm certain that in heaven abortions will be nonexistent since there will be no death. In the eternal state there will be no same-sex marriages—or marriage of any kind for that matter. When Christ reigns over the earth, there will be no need to display the Ten Commandments anywhere, since God's law will be written on the heart of every occupant of heaven. The culture war will eventually be won in the new heaven and the new earth. But the real war that is raging on earth right now is a spiritual war for the eternal souls of every human being. Paul describes our enemy's goal in that war:

And even if our gospel is veiled, it is veiled to those who are perishing, in whose case the god of this world has blinded the minds of the unbelieving so that they might not see the light of the gospel of the glory of Christ, who is the image of God. (2 Corinthians 4:3–4)

Satan, "the god of this world," is working overtime to blind unbelievers to the "light of the gospel" so that they will remain in darkness for all eternity. As those who have been charged with the responsibility to hold out the light of the gospel, we must not diminish or diffuse that light by sacrificing the eternal for the temporal. Curing serious but short-term social ills should never take precedence over healing man's spiritual sickness. After all, cultural maladies are simply symptoms of a much more dangerous disease.

In the pages that follow we will seek to find the balance between standing up for righteousness in order to preserve our culture from premature destruction and shining bright with the unique message of the gospel.

However, don't confuse balance with passivity. Whatever we do, we cannot allow complacency to neutralize our resolve to fight evil or jeopardize our ultimate mission of pointing people to Christ. Remember, being salt and light does not have to be an either/or proposition. As Christians, we must be both.

While it is true that far too many Christians remained silent during the rise of Nazi Germany, there was a remnant of believers who stood tall against the tide of evil without compromising their ultimate message. Albert Einstein, a Jew who was exiled from Germany, made this startling confession about how a small but determined group of believers interested him in Christianity:

> Being a lover of freedom, when the [Nazi] revolution came I looked to the universities to defend it, knowing that they had always boasted of their devotion to the cause of truth; but no, the universities took refuge in silence.
>
> Then I looked to the great editors of the newspapers, whose flaming editorials in days gone by had proclaimed their love of freedom; but they, like the universities, were silenced in a few short weeks.
>
> I then addressed myself to the authors, to those who had passed themselves off as the intellectual guides of Germany, and among whom was frequently discussed the question of freedom and its place in modern life. They are, in turn, very dumb.
>
> Only the Church stood squarely across the path of Hitler's campaign for suppressing the truth. I never had any special in-

terest in the Church before, but now I feel a great affection and admiration for it because the Church alone has had the courage and persistence to stand for intellectual truth and moral freedom. I am forced to confess that what I once despised I now praise unreservedly.[10]

Once again there is a tidal wave of evil that is threatening to overwhelm our country. If we sit on the sidelines, we not only ensure the destruction of our nation but consign countless souls to an eternity of separation from God. It is time for the church to stand up for righteousness and shine brightly with the gospel of Jesus Christ. We must not allow evil to triumph during the twilight years of America.

# CHAPTER
## 2

## When a Nation Implodes

In order to prepare for the construction of our new $130 million church campus in downtown Dallas, our church had to remove six aging buildings that had been part of our campus for many decades. Because these buildings were located in the center of a large city, surrounded by gleaming skyscrapers and adjacent to our historic, 120-year-old church sanctuary, it was imperative that the removal of these buildings be accomplished in a controlled fashion.

The demolition experts explained to me the process of implosion that would collapse 600,000 square feet of buildings in a matter of seconds. "We will strategically place 260 charges utilizing 200 pounds of dynamite throughout the structure. We will then fire these precisely placed demolition charges in a preplanned sequence in specific timed intervals. These sequenced explosives will weaken key support structures, causing the center of the buildings to fall vertically, while at the same time pulling the sides inward. The law of gravity will cause these buildings to collapse under their own weight."

On a brisk fall morning, I stood with the mayor of Dallas and our building committee chairman, along with dozens of members of local and national media, on a rooftop overlooking our soon-to-be-demolished complex. During the previous month 150 workers had been laboring to prepare the buildings for destruction. As a viewing audience of 17 million people from around the world looked on, I made some brief introductory comments and then began the countdown: "Six . . . five . . . four . . . three . . . two . . . one . . . fire!" The mayor, committee chairman, and I pressed the ceremonial red button and the implosions expert radioed to begin the firing sequence.

First, there was a series of loud explosions followed by . . . nothing. Then a second series of explosions followed by . . . more nothing. Knowing that the world was watching, I wondered if what had promised to be an explosive spectacle had turned into a dud. I could see this scene being played endlessly on YouTube.

But within a matter of seconds there began a rumbling vibration we could feel half a block away, followed by a deafening roar that could only be compared to standing next to a jet engine. Suddenly, the buildings began to shake and then collapse both vertically and inwardly, just as the experts had predicted. Within thirty seconds these mighty buildings had been reduced to a plume of debris-filled dust and a pile of rubble.

Looking out over the mass of twisted steel and concrete, I thought of the apostle John's description of the sudden destruction of the future great city of Babylon at the end of the Tribulation. John describes Babylon's leaders' astonishment that such a metropolis could be leveled so quickly:

> And the kings of the earth, who committed acts of immorality and lived sensuously with her, will weep and lament over her when they see the smoke of her burning, standing at a distance because of the fear of her torment, saying, "Woe, woe, the great city, Babylon, the strong city! For in one hour your judgment has come." (Revelation 18:9–10)

Implosions are dramatic. They are over quickly. And they always begin with a series of seemingly unrelated explosions that weaken the infrastructure, causing the building to eventually collapse under its own weight.

A series of bad choices by government leaders has certainly weakened the underlying structure of America. For example, the federal government's failure to adequately protect our borders has made us increasingly vulnerable to terrorist attacks. The four-thousand-mile border between the United States and Canada is one of the longest unguarded frontiers on earth with about one nonmilitary border agent for every ten to fifteen miles.[1] Canada's lax immigration policy coupled with our inadequate border protection make a terrorist's entry into our nation relatively easy.

Additionally, our inspection of imported goods is practically nonexistent. Every year more than six million containers arrive in our country by ship from foreign ports with only 5 percent undergoing inspection. That means that about 5.7 million shipping containers are allowed into our ports each year without any inspection—any one of which could contain a nuclear weapon.[2]

If terrorists don't succeed in leveling one of our cities, then our own politicians seem determined to destroy our economy. Washington's inability to turn off the spending spigot has led to a national debt of nearly $15 trillion. The *New York Times* estimates that the cost for servicing our national debt will be $700 billion annually by 2019.[3] But such figures fail to take into account the unseen but very real financial liabilities that face us through entitlement programs such as Social Security and Medicare, amounting to more than $106 trillion. That means our nation (meaning you, me, our children, and grandchildren) face an indebtedness of $118 trillion, or $383,000 per person.[4] And you thought your Visa bill was a problem!

However, I am not panicked over these security and economic challenges confronting our country. Eventually another terrorist attack will force us to find a way to protect our citizens against those who seek to destroy us. Similarly, I'm confident that another seismic economic event such as the near meltdown of our banking system in 2008 will force our politicians to get our nation's fiscal house in order.

But in the last fifty years there have been three explosive decisions that have weakened the spiritual infrastructure of our nation so severely that our eventual implosion is inevitable. Remember, an implosion begins with a series of explosions that weaken the support system. The explosions are followed by a delay before the structure suddenly and dramatically collapses.

What are these three explosions that make the implosion of our nation inevitable? They are landmark decisions by the Supreme Court—the highest judicial body in our nation—that have determined the direction of our nation more than the influence of any president or the mandates of any Congress.

## ★ Explosion #1: *Engel v. Vitale,* 1962 ★

In the case of *Engel v. Vitale,* the Supreme Court determined that students in New York could no longer recite a simple, twenty-two-word voluntary prayer:

> Almighty God, we acknowledge our dependence upon Thee, and we beg Thy blessings upon us, our parents, our teachers, and our country.

Although this prayer promoted no particular denomination (one person described it as a "to-whomever-it-may-concern" prayer), the Supreme Court declared that the prayer breached the "constitutional wall of separation of church and state."[5] In my book *Outrageous Truth* I discuss the origin of this phrase, which secularists have distorted beyond recognition from its original intent.[6] As we will see in chapter 3, neither our nation's founders nor the earliest courts believed that the First Amendment prohibited government's permission and even preference for Christian expressions of worship.

Ironically, the United States Congress begins every session with a prayer that automatically becomes a part of the *Congressional Record.* However, in 1970 the Supreme Court let stand a lower court ruling declaring the reading of the prayers recorded in the *Congressional Record* by students in school is unconstitutional! Five years after *Engel v. Vitale* the High Court let stand a lower court ruling prohibiting a kindergarten teacher leading her preschoolers in the following prayer:

> We thank you for the flowers so sweet;
> We thank you for the food we eat;

We thank you for the birds that sing;
We thank you for everything.

Although the poem did not mention God, the court concluded that the poem might lead children to think about God, and that would be impermissible! One dissenting justice correctly opined about the judicial overreach of such a decision:

> Thus we are asked as a court to prohibit, not only what these children are saying, but also what . . . the children are *thinking*. . . . One who seeks to convert a child's supposed thought into a violation of the [C]onstitution of the United States is placing a meaning on that historic doctrine which would have surprised the founding fathers.[7]

The *Engel v. Vitale* case cascaded into a number of other decisions by the Supreme Court demonstrating hostility, rather than neutrality, toward expressions of faith in the public arena. In the case of *Abington School District v. Schempp*, the Court outlawed the voluntary reading of a chapter of the Bible by students at the beginning of each school day. Usually, the Court would cite legal precedents for its rulings. But in this case, the court chose to utilize "expert testimony" from a psychologist who claimed that reading the Bible without any comment could endanger a student's mental health:

> If portions of the New Testament were read without explanation, they could be, and . . . had been psychologically harmful to the [children].[8]

Compare this to the Supreme Court's ruling 118 years earlier in *Vidal v. Girard's Executors*, in which the court asked:

Why may not the Bible, and especially the New Testament, without note or comment, be read and taught as a divine revelation in the [school]—its general precepts expounded, its evidences explained and its glorious principles of morality inculcated? . . . Where can the purest principles of morality be learned so clearly or so perfectly as from the New Testament?[9]

The prohibition against voluntary prayers (or poems that might make children think about God), along with the mandate against the voluntary reading of the Bible were just preambles to one of the Supreme Court's most outlandish decisions. For years public schools in Kentucky posted copies of the Ten Commandments in their hallways. There was no requirement that students read the commandments, and no teacher was asked to explain commandments such as "Thou shalt not steal," "Thou shalt not bear false witness against thy neighbor," "Thou shalt not kill," and so on. However, in the 1980 case *Stone v. Graham*, the Supreme Court ruled that posting the Ten Commandments was unconstitutional. Their rationale? If I paraphrased it, I doubt you would believe that I was giving a fair appraisal of the Court's reasoning, so I will allow you to read the opinion for yourself:

If the posted copies of the Ten Commandments are to have any effect at all, it will induce the schoolchildren to read, meditate upon, perhaps venerate and obey, the commandments. . . . This . . . is not a permissible state objective under the Establishment Clause [First Amendment].[10]

The Court is saying that simply displaying the Ten Command-ments might motivate children to actually read the commandments and—heaven forbid—obey the commandments! Is encouraging children to read and obey the Ten Commandments not a permis-sible objective of the government? Remember, 136 years earlier in *Vidal v. Girard's Executors,* the High Court not only assumed that government should sanction the teaching of morality but that such morality should be presented as emanating from the Bible. "Why may not the Bible be taught as divine revelation in the school? Where can the purest principles of morality be learned so clearly?" the Court asked.

In a tragic irony, seventeen years after the Supreme Court's *Stone v. Graham* ruling, a dozen students at Heath High School in Paducah, Kentucky, gathered to pray before classes, just as they did every day. As they closed their prayer time, a fourteen-year-old freshman ap-proached the prayer group and began shooting. Three students died and five others were seriously injured in the hallway of a Kentucky school where the Supreme Court had prohibited the words "Thou shalt not kill" from public display.

Was that simply an unfortunate coincidence? Hardly. God warned Israel repeatedly of the devastating consequences that they would ex-perience if they forsook God and forgot His commandments:

My people are destroyed for lack of knowledge.
Because you have rejected knowledge,
I also will reject you from being My priest.
*Since you have forgotten the law of your God,*
*I also will forget your children.* (Hosea 4:6; emphasis added)

In the Bible the word "forget" does not refer to a simple lapse of memory but a deliberate choice to neglect or turn away from something. God was warning the Northern Kingdom of Israel that because they had chosen to turn away from His laws, a judgment was coming against the Israelites that would reverberate throughout the generations to come. That prophecy was fulfilled in 722 BC when the pagan nation of Assyria invaded Israel and the Northern Kingdom became nothing but a memory.

Let me stop here for a moment and ask a simple question. Do you think God has changed His mind in the last three thousand years concerning what He loves and what He hates? If you believe that God's character is unchangeable, how do you think He feels about a nation that prohibits the mention of His name in public and outlaws the teaching of His laws to the children of that nation? Even if the Supreme Court had correctly interpreted the First Amendment regarding prayer, Bible reading, and the posting of the Ten Commandments (which it didn't, as we will see in chapter 3), would that have persuaded God to change His mind? The prophet Samuel clearly answered that question by observing that God "is not a man that He should change His mind" (1 Samuel 15:29).

Some would counter that the government should simply be neutral about spiritual matters and not promote any one religion. But the idea of religious neutrality is a myth. Turning away from the true God always leads to a turning toward false gods. Through Hosea God reminded the Israelites that forgetting God and His laws was just the first step toward idolatry:

Harlotry, wine and new wine take away the understanding. My people consult their wooden idol, and their diviner's wand informs them; for a spirit of harlotry has led them astray, and they have played the harlot, departing from their God. They offer sacrifices on the tops of the mountains and burn incense on the hills. (Hosea 4:11–13)

Building altars on tops of mountains to worship pagan deities seems far removed from our enlightened culture today—until you read the newspaper. Several years ago the Air Force Academy in Colorado Springs announced that it would move stones to a nearby hilltop in order to facilitate the worship of Wiccans, Druids, and other "earth-centered believers." I responded to the action of the Air Force Academy with an editorial in the online version of the *Washington Post*,[11] in which I recounted the story of King Manasseh, who "did evil in the sight of the LORD. . . . For he rebuilt the high places . . . and he erected altars for Baal and made an Asherah, as Ahab king of Israel had done, and worshiped all the host of heaven and served them" (2 Kings 21:2–3).

What was God's response to Manasseh's desire to lead his nation toward religious inclusiveness? God announced, "Behold, I am bringing such calamity on Jerusalem and Judah, that whoever hears of it, both his ears will tingle" (2 Kings 21:12). God soon delivered on His promise by sending the Babylonians to invade Jerusalem, just as the Assyrians had invaded the Northern Kingdom 140 years earlier. Apparently, God did not fully appreciate the merits of theological diversity!

Although the United States Constitution grants every citizen the freedom to worship—or not worship—as he chooses, our Constitution has in no way changed God's attitude toward any nation that makes a deliberate decision to renounce Him as the only true God and to embrace other gods. And make no mistake about it, the renunciation that began with the 1962 Supreme Court decision banning prayer from schools is gaining momentum.

The Poway Unified School District in San Diego, California, ordered math teacher Brad Johnson to take down two banners with references to God including "In God We Trust" (which appears on our national currency) and "God Bless America" (which is the sign-off phrase in every speech by every American president in recent memory). Johnson's signs had been hanging in his classroom for more than twenty-five years. The school board ordered the removal of the banners because they "over-emphasized" God and "might make a Muslim student uncomfortable." Ironically, the board did not object to images of Buddha and a poster of Muslim leader Malcolm X in other classrooms.[12]

Although New York mayor Michael Bloomberg consistently champions the rights of Muslims to worship in a mosque near Ground Zero, his Education Department has been fighting for more than fifteen years to keep Christian congregations from renting space from schools for Sunday worship in public school auditoriums—despite the fact that the United States Supreme Court has clearly stated that renting government property to religious groups does not violate any laws.[13]

The Hawaii State Legislature designated September 24 as Islam Day to foster awareness of and education about Islam.[14] One can only wonder what day the same legislature will designate as Christian Day.

The University of California Hastings College of Law has threatened to discontinue recognizing the Christian Legal Society as a legitimate student organization with the right to meet on campus because of the group's opposition to homosexuality, which violates the university's antidiscrimination policy. The school informed the student organization: it would lose its recognition because of the school's policy against discrimination based on "race, color, religion, national origin, disability, age, sex, or sexual orientation."

Tom Krattenmaker, writing in *USA Today*, summarizes the real issues in this case which will be heard by the United States Supreme Court:

Does religious freedom include the right to discriminate on the basis of gender, race, or sexuality? Do authorities have the right to foist their values on religious groups through carrots and sticks such as meeting-space privileges and the threat of withholding funds? And, as more conservatives are asking these days, shouldn't that oft-proclaimed liberal principle of "tolerance" also be invoked to the benefit of tradition-minded Christians?[15]

In contrast to the intolerance many universities have toward the beliefs of "tradition-minded Christians," George Washington University is willing to bend over backwards to accommodate the beliefs of Muslim students. In October 2010, GWU opened up Sister Splash, a female-only hour at the pool to accommodate Muslim women. Every week the university plans to close the pool to men and cover the glass door with a dark tarp, giving female Muslim students the chance to swim at their leisure. George Washington University is following the lead of other universities such as Harvard and MIT in giving preferential treatment toward Muslim students.[16] Can you imagine how those same universities would react to a request from a group of Christian women requesting special treatment based on the biblical principle of modesty?

However, God apparently has no appreciation for the merits of religious diversity. The psalmist exclaimed, "Blessed is the nation whose God is the LORD" (Psalm 33:12). God is no respecter of people or nations. The nation that reverences God and His Word will be blessed by God. The nation that rejects God and His Word will be rejected by God. Remember God's words spoken through Hosea? "Since you have forgotten the law of your God, I also will forget your children" (Hosea 4:6).

I realize that suggesting God will curse the nation that sanctions the worship of other gods is anathema in today's culture of diversity. We have been indoctrinated to believe that religious pluralism (the belief that all religious systems are equally valid and none can claim exclusivity) is the great strength of our nation. Secularists applaud the Supreme Court's determined efforts to reverse 150 years of American history in which Christianity was elevated above other religions that the Supreme Court labeled as "imposters."

But what we celebrate as diversity, God condemns as idolatry. The first and greatest commandment was "You shall have no other gods before Me" (Exodus 20:3). As Israel prepared to enter the promised land of Canaan, which was filled with those who worshipped pagan deities, God commanded the Israelites to "put away the foreign gods which are in your midst" (Joshua 24:23). In fact, they were told to not even mention the names of these other gods. Tragically, Israel ignored God's commands and incurred His harshest judgments because of her tolerance for the worship of other deities.

Here is the bottom-line question: Has God changed His mind about idolatry? Has God concluded that the First Amendment should usurp the First Commandment? Does God smile upon our nation when we no longer elevate Him and His Son, Jesus Christ, above other gods?

The answers to those questions are self-evident to anyone who believes in the one true God "with whom there is no variation or shifting shadow" (James 1:17). If God is unchanging, then His attitude toward any nation that rejects Him and His Word is also unchanging, which makes America's coming night inevitable.

## ★ Explosion #2: *Roe v. Wade*, 1973 ★

God's special love and concern for children is well documented in Scripture. Jesus demonstrated affection for children and even implied that God appoints angels to watch over them. The Lord warned of the fate of those who harmed a child: "it would be better for him to have a heavy millstone hung around his neck, and to be drowned in the depth of the sea" (Matthew 18:6).

God's love for children explains His burning anger against those in the Old Testament who worshipped the pagan deity Molech. God warned the Israelites that when they entered into Canaan they would encounter the Ammonites, who were worshippers of Molech. But instead of destroying the altars to this detestable deity, some of the Israelites, including King Solomon, embraced the worship of this false god (1 Kings 11:7). What was God's reaction to the Israelites' worship of Molech?

> They [the Israelites] built the high places of Baal that are in the valley of Ben-hinnom to cause their sons and their daughters to pass through the fire to Molech, which I had not commanded them nor had it entered My mind that they should do this abomination, to cause Judah to sin. . . . Behold, I will gather them out of all the lands to which I have driven them in My anger. (Jeremiah 32:35, 37)

God was so repulsed by Israel's worship of Molech that He used the pagan nation of Babylon to bring judgment against His own people.

What made the worship of Molech especially repugnant to God was that it required children "to pass through the fire." The term *pass through the fire* is a reference to a particularly horrific type of child sacrifice. According to some rabbinic writers, the Israelites made a hollow bronze statue to Molech. The idol was in the form of a human but had the head of an ox. Children were placed in the hollow structure and a fire was lit below the idol. Once the fire began to rage, the pagan worshippers would beat their drums louder and louder to drown out the cries of the children who were being burned alive.

You can now understand God's decisive and devastating judgment against Israel for engaging in the worship of Molech. The agonizingly painful process of burning alive is incomprehensible, especially when it involves children. What kind of people would practice such cruelty? Some would argue that it's the same kind of people who engage in abortion, including the especially hideous practice of partial-birth abortions.

The Supreme Court case *Roe v. Wade* (1973) is often credited as the decision that allowed women to have abortions. A companion case that same year, *Doe v. Bolton*, actually expanded that right by mandating a health exception that allows abortions for any reason: physical, psychological, or emotional. This health exception has become the standard by which the Court judges the constitutionality of any law attempting to restrict abortions. For example, in 2003 a US District Court judge ruled that a New Hampshire law requiring parental notification for a minor child receiving an abortion was unconstitutional because there was no health exception to that state law. Such an exception would allow an abortion practitioner to bypass notifying a fourteen-year-old girl's parents that she is having her unborn child killed simply by saying that the teenager's emotional health would be jeopardized by having the child. After several years of court challenges, the parental notification law was repealed completely by New Hampshire voters in 2007. Obviously the health exception clause is wide enough to drive a Mack truck through, allowing for an abortion for any reason at all.

The health exception clause is also being used to open the door to the most heinous type of abortion imaginable: the partial-birth abortion. In the case of *Stenberg v. Carhart* (2000), the Supreme Court struck down a Nebraska law banning partial-birth abortions because it did not contain a health exception clause.

What makes partial-birth abortions so barbaric? Dr. Stephen Chasen, associate professor of obstetrics and gynecology at the Weill Medical College of Cornell University, is one of the plaintiffs against the Partial-Birth Abortion Ban Act, signed by President George W. Bush in 2003 and unsuccessfully challenged by Planned Parenthood, the National Abortion Federation, and a number of other pro-abortion lobbyists.

In one of the suits challenging the ban on partial-birth abortions, Dr. Chasen was questioned by the government about the nature of this procedure:

**The Court:**     You wrap a small sterile towel around the fetus, because it is slippery, and after the legs are out you pull on the sacrum, or the lower portion of the spine, to continue to remove the fetus, right?

**The Witness:**  Right.

**The Court:**     When the fetus is out of the level of the breech, you place another, larger towel around the first small towel, right?

**The Witness:**  Right.

**The Court:**     You gently pull downward on the sacrum until the shoulder blades appear, right?

**The Witness:**  Right. . . .

**The Court:**    Then the fetus is at a point where only the head remains in the cervix, correct?

**The Witness:**  That's correct.

[At this point the government asks what happens if the fetus's head will not fit out intact due to gestational age or the amount of cervical dilation.]

**The Court:**    If you can't do that, you know you are going to have to crush the head, and so you take a clamp and you grasp the cervix to elevate it, and then your assistant there in the operating room will pull down on the fetus's legs or back, gently lowering the fetus's head toward the opening of the vagina, right?

**The Witness:**  Right.

**The Court:**    That is when you put two fingers at the back of the fetus's neck at the base of the skull where you can feel the base of the skull, and then you puncture the skull with the scissors, right?

**The Witness:**  I can usually see it as well as feel it. But yes.

**The Court:**    At that point you see some brain tissue come out, and you are 100 percent certain that you are in the brain, so you open the scissors to expand the hole, remove the scissors, and put the suction device in the skull, right?

**The Witness:**  Correct.

**The Court:**    You turn on the suction, and typically the fetus comes right out with the suction device still in its skull, right?

**The Witness:**  Right.[17]

Remember, the above doctor describing this horrendous act is speaking *in favor* of the procedure!

Those who oppose any kind of ban on partial-birth abortions claim that this procedure is extremely rare and when it is performed, it usually occurs early in a pregnancy. Both claims are false. In 1997 the executive director of the National Coalition of Abortion Providers admitted that partial-birth abortions were common and that they were usually done on a healthy mother carrying a healthy fetus that was twenty or more weeks old.[18]

Can the fetus feel the pain of having its skull punctured and crushed? Dr. Carolyn Westhoff, professor of epidemiology and population and family health at Columbia University, testified that there is "usually a heartbeat" when she collapses the skull of the fetus during a partial-birth abortion. Regarding the possibility of fetal pain, Dr. Westhoff testified, "I do know that when we do, for instance, an amniocentesis and put a needle through the abdomen into the amniotic cavity that the fetus withdraws, so I certainly know based on my experience that the fetus [will] withdraw in response [to] a painful stimulus."[19]

But to those proponents of partial-birth abortions, the pain a fetus feels is immaterial compared to a mother's "right" to kill her child, as evidenced by this amazing admission by Dr. Chasen during cross-examination by the judge in one of the cases challenging the ban on partial-birth abortions:

**The Court:**    Does it hurt the baby?
**The Witness:**  I don't know.
**The Court:**    But you go ahead and do it anyway, is that right?
**The Witness:**  I am taking care of my patients, and in that process, yes, I go ahead and do it.

| | |
|---|---|
| **The Court:** | Does that mean you take care of your patient and the baby be damned, is that the approach you have? |
| **The Witness:** | These women who are having [abortions] at gestational ages . . . are legally entitled to it— |
| **The Court:** | I didn't ask you that, Doctor. I asked you if you had any care or concern for the fetus whose head you were crushing. |
| **The Witness:** | No.[20] |

Fortunately, in April 2007 the United States Supreme Court in a 5–4 decision narrowly upheld the constitutionality of the Partial-Birth Abortion Ban signed by President George W. Bush, without requiring a health exception. But the current administration, led by President Obama, has protested the Court's decision. While running for his first term as president, Barack Obama decried the Court's decision to uphold the ban on partial-birth abortions in a speech before Planned Parenthood in July 2007: "There's a lot at stake in this election, especially for our daughters. To appreciate that all you have to do is review the recent decisions handed down by the Supreme Court of the United States. For the first time . . . the Supreme Court upheld a federal ban on abortions with criminal penalties for doctors," the president lamented. "Some people argue that the federal ban on abortion was just an isolated effort aimed at one medical procedure—that it's not a part of a concerted effort to roll back the hard-won rights of American women. That presumption is also wrong," Obama claimed.[21]

On the thirty-fifth anniversary of *Roe v. Wade*, then-presidential candidate Barack Obama pledged that if elected president he would appoint Supreme Court justices who would vote to ban restrictions on abortion, including partial-birth abortions. "Thirty-five years after the Supreme Court decided *Roe v. Wade*, it's never been more important to protect a woman's right to choose," Obama declared. "Last year, the Supreme Court decided by a vote of 5–4 to uphold the Federal Abortion Ban, and in doing so undermined an important principle of *Roe v. Wade*: that we must always protect women's health. With one more vacancy on the Supreme Court, we could be looking at a majority hostile to a women's fundamental right to choose for the first time since *Roe v. Wade*. The next president may be asked to nominate that Supreme Court justice. That is what is at stake in this election."[22]

Then-candidate Barack Obama got one thing right. The next president would make appointment(s) to the Supreme Court that could determine the fate of legalized abortion, including partial-birth abortions, in America. Obama won the presidential election in 2008 and has already appointed two justices (Sonia Sotomayor and Elena Kagan) who appear resolute on maintaining *Roe v. Wade*. Many believe that whoever is elected president in 2012 and in subsequent elections could make several more appointments to the High Court and thus tip the Court decisively toward or against the protection of the unborn for decades to come.

No one doubts which direction President Obama will lean if reelected in 2012. By his actions and by his words, Obama has demonstrated his unequivocal support for a woman's right to choose . . . to murder her unborn child. (Why are abortion proponents unwilling to complete that sentence?) In 1997, Obama voted in the Illinois Senate against SB 230, a bill designed to prevent partial-birth abortions. On March 30, 2001, Obama was the only Illinois senator who rose to speak against a bill that would have protected babies who survived late term labor-induced abortion.

Amazingly, Obama prides himself on championing choice . . . the choice to kill an unborn child. During his run for president in 2008, Obama boasted, "Throughout my career I've been a consistent and strong supporter of reproductive justice, and have consistently had a 100% pro-choice rating with Planned Parenthood and NARAL Pro-Choice America."[23]

Since 1973 when the highest court in America declared that abortion was legal, nearly fifty million unborn children have been murdered, and an additional 1.3 million children are being killed each year. Stop for a moment and allow those numbers to sink in. Fifty million people represents nearly one-fifth of our entire population! What are the implications of the slaughter of so many people in less than fifty years, as well as the continuing effects of wiping out so many children who would eventually grow into productive members of society?

### ★ Social Insecurity ★

One of the infrequently mentioned effects of abortion is its economic impact on our nation. The underlying foundation of our economic prosperity is consumerism. Approximately two-thirds of all economic activity in the United States comes from consumer spending, which in turn is dependent upon population growth. In an article titled "The $35 Trillion Elephant in the Room," Dennis Howard writes, "We found that the 50.5 million surgical abortions since 1970 have cost the U.S. an astonishing $35 trillion in lost Gross Domestic Product. . . . If you include all the babies lost to IUDs, RU-486, sterilization, and abortifacients, the number climbs to $70 trillion!"[24]

Writer Laura Antikowiak links the current funding crisis facing

Social Security and Medicare to abortion. The loss of fifty million children in fifty years means there will be fewer young people to care for those preparing for retirement. This is catastrophic for a system that is built on one generation's retirement being paid for by a younger, working generation's taxes. Antikowiak predicts, "Unless we raise taxes, cut benefits, or overhaul the entire system, Medicare will be bankrupt in the 2020s and Social Security in the 2030s." She calculates that in 1998 alone, the aborted babies who were victims of *Roe v. Wade* would have contributed approximately $1.7 billion to Medicare and $7.4 billion to Social Security—enough to cover the average monthly benefit of 785,000 retired workers for an entire year![25]

While the economic loss from infanticide is substantial, it pales in comparison to the most serious result of abortion: the guarantee of God's judgment. One only has to look at history to see how God deals with nations that murder children. He raised up the Babylonians and Assyrians to invade Israel for practicing child sacrifice. God used the Allied Forces to crush Nazi Germany for sending children by the trainloads to the gas chambers. Do we really have to wonder about God's attitude toward a nation like ours that sanctions the killing of tens of millions of children?

## ★ Explosion #3: *Lawrence and Garner v. Texas* (2003) ★

You may not be familiar with this Supreme Court case, but the social and moral implications of *Lawrence and Garner v. Texas* are just as serious as the other two judicial explosions already discussed. Let's look at the details of the case.

Responding to a reported weapons disturbance in a private residence in Houston, police entered the apartment of John Lawrence and saw him engaging in a sexual act with another man, Tyron Garner. Both men were arrested and convicted of violating a Texas statute forbidding two persons of the same gender engaging in certain sexual acts (sodomy). The High Court was asked to decide whether laws forbidding consensual sex among persons of the same gender violated the Constitution's guarantee of equal protection of the law. In a 6–3 ruling, the Supreme Court declared the Texas anti-sodomy statute unconstitutional. Justice Anthony Kennedy, writing the majority opinion, stated, "[The two men's] right to liberty under the Due Process Clause gives them the full right to engage in their conduct without intervention of the government. The Texas statute furthers no legitimate state interest which can justify its intrusion into the personal and private life of the individual."[26]

Even some conservatives have a difficult time being alarmed over the *Lawrence* decision. After all, even though we may personally deem homosexuality to be immoral, do we really want the government legislating our behavior in the bedroom? Isn't less governmental interference the bedrock belief of conservatism? The thought of policemen entering our homes in the middle of the night—as they did in the situation spawning the *Lawrence* case—and arresting citizens for sexual behavior the state finds objectionable is a frightening thought to many. Indeed, even Justice Clarence Thomas, who voted to uphold the Texas law prohibiting sodomy, termed such statutes as "silly laws."

However, what we term "silly," God considers serious. The Bible consistently forbids homosexual activity:

You shall not lie with a male as one lies with a female; it is an abomination. (Leviticus 18:22)

If there is a man who lies with a male as those who lie with a woman, both of them have committed a detestable act; they shall surely be put to death. Their bloodguiltiness is upon them. (Leviticus 20:13)

Some argue that these prohibitions were unique to Israel and part of the Mosaic law, which also forbade the breeding of two different kinds of cattle and the wearing of two kinds of material (Leviticus 19:19). Since we no longer consider those latter laws relevant, shouldn't we also discard the commands against homosexuality?

However, the laws against homosexuality are not limited to the Old Testament law for Israel. The New Testament also contains numerous prohibitions against homosexuality:

For this reason God gave them over to degrading passions; for their women exchanged the natural function for that which is unnatural, and in the same way also the men abandoned the natural function of the woman and burned in their desire toward one another, men with men committing indecent acts and receiving in their own persons the due penalty of their error. (Romans 1:26–27)

Or do you not know that the unrighteous will not inherit the kingdom of God? Do not be deceived; neither fornicators, nor idolaters, nor adulterers, nor effeminate, *nor homosexuals*, nor thieves, nor the covetous, nor drunkards, nor revilers, nor swindlers, will inherit the kingdom of God. (1 Corinthians 6:9–10; emphasis added)

But we know that the Law is good, if one uses it lawfully, realizing the fact that law is not made for a righteous person, but for those who are lawless and rebellious, for the ungodly and sinners, for the unholy and profane, for those who kill their fathers or mothers, for murderers and immoral men and *homosexuals* and kidnappers and liars and perjurers, and whatever else is contrary to sound teaching. (1 Timothy 1:8–10; emphasis added)

There are numerous reasons that God has included such "silly laws" in His Word. One stated rationale for prohibiting homosexuality is that it is "unnatural," as Paul describes it in Romans 1:26. The word *unnatural* in this passage means "against nature." God is the One who originally thought up the idea of sexual intercourse. Now take a moment and allow that thought to sink in! One day God was sitting in heaven and thought to Himself, *Wouldn't this be a fun thing for human beings to do with one another?* God then took out a sketch pad and designed the biological equipment needed for His creatures to enjoy themselves and experience the physical, emotional, and spiritual oneness He desired between a husband and his wife. God then gave His creatures an instruction manual for how to use the equipment for optimal benefit. Included in that manual were some warnings from the Manufacturer about sexual behavior that would be harmful to the user: sex before marriage, sex with another partner during marriage, and sex with someone of the same gender.

Just as plugging a toaster designed to operate at 120 volts into a 220 outlet will ruin the appliance, we should not be surprised that misuse of our sexual faculties can also result in serious physical consequences. Since the Bible categorizes homosexual acts as the misuse of one's sexual organs, it stands to reason that there would be attendant physical illnesses associated with such behavior. And there are.

The link between homosexual activity and sexually transmitted diseases, as well as other physical maladies, is well documented. The gay newspaper the *Washington Blade* reported in 2009 that "Gay and bisexual men account for half of new HIV infections in the U.S. and have AIDS at a rate more than 50 times greater than other groups, according to Centers for Disease Control & Prevention data."[27]

Through 2007, AIDS took the lives of 274,184 American men whose only known risk factor was that they had engaged in sex with other men.[28] Those who insist that AIDS is just as prevalent among heterosexuals as homosexuals and is contracted as easily from blood transfusions as from gay intercourse do not have the facts. AIDS is primarily a homosexual disease. Matt Foreman, the executive director of the National Gay and Lesbian Task Force, made that stunning admission to a group of homosexual activists on February 8, 2008: "Folks, with 70 percent of the people in this country living with HIV being gay or bi[sexual], we cannot deny that HIV is a gay disease. We have to own that and face up to that."[29]

While AIDS is the most serious of diseases associated with homosexual behavior, it is not the only one. The Centers for Disease Control and Prevention warns, "Men who have sex with men (MSM) are at elevated risk for certain sexually transmitted diseases (STDs), including Hepatitis A, Hepatitis B, HIV/AIDS, syphilis, gonorrhea, and chlamydia."[30] The *Archives of Internal Medicine* reports that homosexuals acquire syphilis at a rate ten times that of heterosexuals.[31] Furthermore, unnatural sexual acts engaged in by homosexuals cause other serious illnesses.[32]

God had His reasons for including in His Word "silly laws" forbidding homosexual acts. As our Creator, He knew from the beginning the serious health risks of misusing our bodies, which He designed.

I think it is ironic that while many people react violently against any governmental attempt to regulate sexual practices, we readily accept other government statutes such as requiring seat belts for drivers and helmets for motorcyclists. Although such laws regulate private behavior, the government has determined that they protect society as a whole against wasteful medical costs and unnecessary deaths.

Yet the health risks associated with homosexual acts are just as serious and costly as those posed by not wearing seat belts or helmets. Taxpayers through Medicaid foot the bill for at least 50 percent of all people diagnosed with HIV/AIDS, 90 percent of children with HIV/AIDS, and 70 percent of women with HIV/AIDS. The lifetime medical cost for treating a person with HIV/AIDS from infection until death is estimated at $154,402 for adults and $491,936 for children.[33]

But the societal ramifications of the Supreme Court's *Lawrence* decision extend far beyond government approval of homosexual activity. The Supreme Court believes that implicit in the Fourteenth Amendment of the Constitution is the right of every American to engage in whatever kind of sexual behavior he or she desires." Justice Kennedy, writing for the Court in Lawrence, states, "Our laws and tradition afford constitutional protection to personal decisions relating to marriage, procreation, contraception, family relationships, child rearing, and education. . . . Persons in a homosexual relationship may seek autonomy for these purposes, just as heterosexual persons do."[34]

If that is true, then it is not difficult to identify the next moral domino that is about to fall: state laws banning homosexual marriages. After all, what right does the state have to deprive two men or two women expressing their love for one another through the institution of marriage? Supreme Court Justice Antonin Scalia, writing for the three dissenting justices in the *Lawrence* case, opined, "This reasoning leaves on pretty shaky grounds state laws limiting marriage to opposite-sex couples."[35] After the *Lawrence* decision, professor and gay rights activists Chai Feldblum predicted, "The Court will be ready to recognize marriage for gay people when the general public believes that the union of two gay people is morally similar to the union of two heterosexual people. . . . And I think we're closer to that than I would have anticipated five years ago."[36]

If Feldblum is correct that the Supreme Court's recognition of homosexual marriage hinges on public acceptance, then we may be closer than even Feldblum believes. In 1996 only 27 percent of the population favored same-sex marriage. According to a May 2011 poll, 53 percent of citizens in the United States favor it.[37] Even more alarming is the growing approval among young evangelical Christians of gay marriage. According to a Beliefnet survey in 2008, 61.8 percent of the oldest group of evangelicals surveyed said "stopping gay marriage" was very important, while only 34 percent of the younger group agreed.[38] Furthermore, a Pew Religion Forum survey in 2008 found that young evangelicals are more than twice as likely (24 percent versus 10 percent) as their older counterparts to support gay couples being allowed to marry, and another 32 percent supports only civil unions. That means that 58 percent of young evangelical Christians surveyed support some kind of legal recognition of gay partnerships.[39]

The student newspaper of my alma mater, Baylor University (a Texas Baptist institution), published an editorial supporting homosexual marriage. The editors of the *Lariat* wrote, "Like many heterosexual couples, many gay couples share deep bonds of love, some so strong they've persevered years of discrimination for their choice to co-habitate with and date one another. Just as it isn't fair to discriminate against someone for their skin color, heritage or religious beliefs, it isn't fair to discriminate against someone for their sexual orientation. Shouldn't gay couples be allowed to enjoy the benefits and happiness of marriage, too?"[40]

When even evangelical Christians are caving in to societal pressures to embrace homosexual unions, the Supreme Court's acceptance of gay marriage can't be far behind. As I type these words, California's Proposition 8 banning gay marriage is on its way to a hearing before the Supreme Court. If the Court uses the same logic as it did in the *Lawrence* case, it is inevitable that they will strike down all state laws forbidding homosexual marriage.

You may be thinking, *So what? How does the legitimization of homosexual marriage hurt society?* First, redefining marriage to include same-sex relationships devalues the institution of marriage. For example, suppose that society determined that the word *purple* should no longer be restricted to describing what has been traditionally thought of as the color purple, but instead, *purple* should now be used to describe every hue and tint in the earth. An apple, a daisy, and the sky are all declared to be *purple*. Suddenly, the color purple has lost its distinctiveness. In a world where everything is purple, nothing is truly purple.

If we start describing an immoral relationship between two men or two women as marriage, why stop there? Suppose three men and a woman or a man and his nineteen-year-old daughter decide they want to be married; why should they be denied that right? I once made that argument on Fox News's *The O'Reilly Factor*. The man I was debating called such reasoning "ridiculous" but could offer no counterargument—because there is none.

In reality, surveys reveal that not that many homosexual couples desire marriage. The real damage of legitimization of same-sex marriages is what it does to devalue heterosexual marriages. Stanley

Kurtz, a senior fellow at The Hoover Institute of Stanford University, contends that the legitimization of same-sex unions in Scandinavian countries has caused the marriage rate to drop dramatically, while the number of children born out of wedlock has risen.[41] People reasoned that if marriage could be redefined to include any and every relationship, then why bother to marry at all?

The redefinition and resulting devaluing of marriage has devastating effects on children. Although it is not always possible, a child reared in a nuclear family with his father and mother will fare better than those reared in a nontraditional family (homosexual unions or single-parent homes). The National Longitudinal Survey of Adolescent Health has found that . . .

- Adolescents in intact families, as a group, are the least likely to feel depressed.
- The national average grade-point scores of children in intact families are higher than those children living in nontraditional families.
- The rate of youth incarceration is significantly greater for children raised in nontraditional families.[42]

Regardless of the claims that homosexual couples can be effective parents, the truth is that a child needs both his biological father and mother to ensure his well-being. Sara McLanahan, a sociologist from Princeton University, has written:

If we were asked to design a system for making sure that children's basic needs were met, we would probably come up with something quite similar to the two-parent family ideal. . . . The fact that both parents have a biological connection to the child would increase the likelihood that the parents would identify with the child and be willing to sacrifice for that child, and it would reduce the likelihood that either parent would abuse the child.[43]

The assertion that children reared by a homosexual couple fare just as well as those reared by heterosexual couples is a myth. David Popenoe writes about the effects of children in fatherless homes (remember, the majority of homosexuals who rear children are lesbians). Seventy percent of long-term prison inmates grew up in fatherless homes, as did 60 percent of rapists and 72 percent of adolescent murderers.[44]

Both fathers and mothers are necessary for successfully rearing children. Read McLanahan's statement again: "If we were asked to design a system for making sure that children's basic needs were met, we would probably come up with something quite similar to the two-parent family ideal." I wonder if she understood the irony of her words? Our Creator has already designed the optimum structure for the rearing of children: one man and one woman committed in marriage to one another for life. It's called the family. And although circumstances beyond our control, such as unwanted divorce or death, can change the dynamics of a home, Jesus reminds us that the idea of a man and woman united together for a lifetime was God's plan from the beginning:

Have you not read that He who created them from the beginning MADE THEM MALE AND FEMALE, and said, "FOR THIS REASON A MAN SHALL LEAVE HIS FATHER AND MOTHER AND BE JOINED TO HIS WIFE, AND THE TWO SHALL BECOME ONE FLESH"? So they are no longer two, but one flesh. What therefore God has joined together, let no man separate. (Matthew 19:4–6)

For the first 226 years of our nation's history, our judiciary recognized the relationship between the divine (and therefore, historic) definition of the family and social order. James Kent, who served as chief justice of the New York Supreme Court, wrote in his commentary on American law, "The primary and most important of the domestic relations, is that of husband and wife. It has its foundation in nature, and is the only relation by which Providence has permitted the continuance of the human race. . . . It is one of the chief foundations of social order."[45]

In the case of *Murphy v. Ramsey* (1885), the U.S. Supreme Court observed that

no legislation could be "more wholesome and necessary" in the founding of a "free, self-governing commonwealth" than that which sees the family "as consisting in and springing from the union for life of one man and one woman in the holy estate of matrimony." This family model would be "the best guaranty of that reverent morality which is the source of all beneficent progress in social and political improvement."[46]

As late as the mid-twentieth century, the courts understood the importance of supporting the historic understanding of the family. California Supreme Court Justice Roger Traynor researched the decisions of extant Supreme Court decisions and summarized the place of the family in American law. "The family is the basic unit of our society, the center of the personal affections that ennoble and enrich human life. It channels biological drives that might otherwise become socially destructive; it ensures the care and education of children in a stable environment; it establishes continuity from one generation to another; it nurtures and develops the individual initiative that distinguishes a free people."[47]

Yet the *Lawrence* decision in 2003 has opened the door to what both conservatives and liberals agree is an inevitable redefinition of marriage. Don't let anyone mislead you. This fervor to redesign the most basic social structure in society is fueled by sexual perversion that is motivated by a rebellion against God, according to the apostle Paul:

> For they exchanged the truth of God for a lie. . . . For this reason God gave them over to degrading passions; for their women exchanged the natural function for that which is unnatural, and in the same way also the men abandoned the natural function of the woman and burned in their desire toward one another, men with men committing indecent acts and receiving in their own persons the due penalty of their error. (Romans 1:25–27)

What happens to a nation that rebels against God and discards His design for the most basic social structure in society? Sometimes God judges without delay as He did with the cities of Sodom and Gomorrah. Although the Bible cites a number of sins for which the cities were known, it was sexual immorality—specifically homosexuality—that caused God to rain fire and brimstone upon them and destroy them instantly:

> Just as Sodom and Gomorrah and the cities around them, since they in the same way as these indulged in gross immorality and went after strange flesh [literally, "going after that which is not natural"], are exhibited as an example in undergoing the punishment of eternal fire. (Jude v. 7)

However, other times there is delay between explosive choices a society makes and the natural collapse that comes from removing the spiritual and moral support structures of a society, just as there is with an implosion.

You and I are living in that pause in history between explosion and implosion. Such a realization should not drive us to panic but fill us with hope! Why? If indeed we are in America's twilight, then a time of darkness is soon approaching. But nighttime doesn't last forever. The night is always followed by the breaking of a new dawn.

That was God's message to the Israelites during Judah's twilight. Through the prophet Jeremiah, God warned the nation that because of her disobedience her implosion was imminent. But God also looked beyond the seventy years of severe judgment Judah would experience and assured His people that a brighter day was coming:

"For I know the plans that I have for you," declares the LORD, "plans for welfare and not for calamity to give you a future and a hope." (Jeremiah 29:11)

Our future hope is that the coming darkness that will engulf America and every other nation in the world will be followed by the dawn of Christ's return, when He will establish a new heaven and a new earth. But until that time, God has left us on earth during these twilight years for a very specific purpose that we will explore in the pages that follow.

# CHAPTER
# 3

## The Most Misunderstood Word in America

Tolerance is a virtue for the man with no convictions," wrote G. K. Chesterton.[1] Chesterton's observation helps explain the inverse relationship between the embracing of tolerance and the rejection of absolute moral standards in our culture. Listen closely to the voices around you, and you will conclude that tolerance is the most important character quality that can be developed. The conviction that all beliefs and behaviors are equally valid is celebrated as the highest ideal in our culture. In Ayn Rand's novel *The Fountainhead*, Dominique Francon claims, ". . . we must have tolerance for the opinions of others, because tolerance is the greatest virtue."[2] As author and social critic Os Guinness observed, "Ours then is a world in which 'Thou shalt not judge' has become the new eleventh commandment, and tolerance the last undisputed virtue."[3]

The elevation of tolerance over truth is not accidental. Many educators believe that encouraging tolerance of all beliefs and behaviors should be the ultimate objective for teaching. The Southern Poverty Law Center publishes a magazine called *Teaching Tolerance* (offered free to school teachers and administrators). At one time, the organization's website stated:

> Tolerance is an idea that is universally relevant, and it belongs everywhere in the curriculum. Here you will read about teachers and students working together to improve race relations, respect religious diversity and ability differences, dispel gender bias and homophobia, confront hate and build classroom community.[4]

Lest you think this is an isolated example used to support a hyperbolic statement about the worship of tolerance in our educational system, read carefully these words by Stephen Bates from *The American Enterprise*:

> Tolerance may indeed be the dominant theme of the modern curriculum. The authors of a recent study of American high schools concluded "tolerating diversity is the moral glue that holds schools together." One study of American history books found toleration presented as "the only 'religious' idea worth remembering."[5]

The effort by educators to indoctrinate students to embrace tolerance is having a profound effect on our beliefs. The worship of tolerance has led to an increasing acceptance of those practices once believed to be morally wrong. A Gallup poll has recorded a general increase over the last thirty years of those who believe homosexual relationships should be legal (59 percent) and that sex between an unmarried man and woman (59 percent), divorce (65 percent), and having a baby out of wedlock (54 percent) are morally acceptable.[6]

My real concern, however, is not with the changing values of the overall population, but with the growing number of evangelical Christians who have concluded that all beliefs and behaviors are equally valid. A 2008 poll of thirty-five thousand Americans revealed that "57 percent of evangelical church attenders said they believe that many religions can lead to eternal life."[7] A poll by George Barna a few years ago discovered that the majority of those identifying themselves as born-again Christian adults and 76 percent of Christian teenagers rejected the concept of absolute truth—the idea that there are principles that apply to everyone regardless of their culture or personal belief system.[8] The result of rejecting absolute truth is embracing relativism, a philosophy that is best expressed by the simple dictum "Everything is right sometime, and nothing is right every time."

What is the net result of Christians embracing relativism? We become tasteless salt and a diminished light. For example, if we do not really believe that abortion is tantamount to murder, why insist that the candidates we elect be pro-life? If we are not convinced that homosexuality is a perversion, why would we oppose efforts to teach schoolchildren that homosexuality is an acceptable lifestyle choice? Once we buy into the concept of relativism, we will quickly lose any motivation to stand up against the tide of immorality that is threatening to engulf our culture. To carry forward the imagery from the last chapter, why stand in front of a crumbling Hoover Dam if you aren't convinced that a flood is a bad thing? When Christians lose their motivation to be restrainers of evil, it is only a matter of time until society crumbles under the weight of its own sin. Jesus said it this way:

You are the salt of the earth; but if the salt has become tasteless, how can it be made salty again? It is no longer good for anything, except to be thrown out and trampled under foot by men. (Matthew 5:13)

Relativism also dims a Christian's light. Media entrepreneur Oprah Winfrey claims to be a Christian. However, she does not believe that Christianity's truth is exclusive. "One of the biggest mistakes humans make is to believe there is only one way. Actually, there are many diverse paths leading to what you call God."[9] Of course, her conviction that other religious belief systems are just as valid as her own (whatever that may be) contradicts the words of the Founder of her faith, Jesus Christ, who proclaimed "I am the way, and the truth, and the life; no one comes to the Father but through Me" (John 14:6). Unfortunately, if the Barna poll cited earlier is correct, more Christians believe Oprah Winfrey than Jesus Christ.

The most obvious result of believing that all religions offer an equally valid pathway to God is a loss of motivation to encourage people of different faiths or no faith to trust in Jesus Christ for their salvation. Dr. Roy Fish, retired professor of evangelism at Southwestern Baptist Theological Seminary, laments the decline in personal evangelism in a denomination long-noted for its efforts in that area. When the Southern Baptist Convention had eight million members back in the 1950s, it took about twenty Baptists a whole year to win one person to faith in Christ. Today, with a membership of over sixteen million people, it takes forty-four church members to lead someone to Christ.[10]

Fish believes that spiritual relativism is a primary culprit in the loss of evangelistic zeal. "Very little will stultify evangelism and missions any quicker than the belief that nobody is really lost and everybody is going to make it to heaven sooner or later. . . . Why go across the sea . . . or across the street with the message of Jesus if everybody is either already saved or everybody will make it to heaven . . . anyhow?"[11]

In Matthew 5:15 Jesus observed that it was unthinkable to "light a lamp and put it under a basket." Such a light would be unseen and, therefore, useless. Spiritual relativism has the same effect on the gospel of Jesus Christ. If Christians believe that all religions illuminate equally valid paths to God, then they will have little motivation to hold out the light of Jesus Christ and say, "Here is the only way to find God." The net result of spiritual relativism is a hidden gospel.

## ★ A Most Misunderstood Word ★

Up to this point we have equated *tolerance* with *relativism*. In today's world people commonly believe that tolerance requires the rejection of any moral or spiritual absolutes. If someone says, "I am tolerant of homosexuality," we assume he means that he has no strong persuasion that such behavior is evil. If someone professes to be tolerant of all religions, we presume that he probably does not believe there is only one way to God. We conclude that a truly tolerant person is one who responds to every controversial truth claim with an easygoing "whatever."

However, what I call true tolerance not only allows, but *requires* a belief in absolute truth. Author Gregory Kouki notes, "Probably no concept has more currency in our politically correct culture than the notion of tolerance. Unfortunately, one of America's noblest virtues has been so distorted it's become a vice."[12] I must confess that I have been guilty at times of disparaging the noble concept of tolerance because I have failed to distinguish between true tolerance and pseudotolerance. To understand the distortion of the meaning of tolerance, we need to recover the original understanding of this very worthy ideal.

Many years ago, my grandmother wrote a poem titled "A Plea for Tolerance." However, my grandmother's understanding of tolerance varied greatly from today's popular understanding of the word. The historic understanding of tolerance is best understood from *Webster's New World Dictionary*, Second College Edition: "To allow or to permit, to recognize and respect others' beliefs and practices without sharing them, to bear or put up with someone or something not necessarily liked."[13]

Gregory Kouki identifies the three critical components of historic (or "true") tolerance: 1) permitting or allowing, 2) a conduct or point of view one disagrees with, 3) while respecting the person in the process.[14]

Here is the obvious but universally overlooked component of tolerance: "a conduct or point of view *one disagrees with*." You can only truly be tolerant of someone or something with which you disagree. For example, suppose I'm invited to a banquet and the dessert served is Häagen-Dazs vanilla ice cream topped with chocolate sauce—which just happens to be my favorite dessert.

If my wife asked me, "How did you like your dessert?" would I respond, "I tolerated it"? Since I probably would have just about licked the bowl clean, that would hardly be an accurate response! However, if the dessert were key lime pie (my least favorite dessert), I might feel obligated to nibble at it out of politeness to my host. Thus,

"I tolerated dessert" would be an accurate description of my attitude and actions regarding the key lime pie. Using Kouki's three components of tolerance:

1. I permitted the pie to be served to me (rather than throwing it across the room).
2. Nevertheless, I did not change my mind that it was a poor dessert selection.
3. I was still gracious to the host who invited me.

## ★ Pseudotolerance ★

The concept of tolerance has undergone a radical metamorphosis. To most people tolerance requires the acceptance of all ideas and behavior as equally truthful and acceptable, such as:

- Hinduism and Christianity are equally valid belief systems.
- Heterosexuality and homosexuality are equally valid expressions of human sexuality.
- Choosing to abort a child or choosing to keep a child are equally valid moral choices, depending upon the particular circumstances.
- Cohabitation and marriage are equally valid options in a relationship.
- Key lime pie and Häagen-Dazs vanilla ice cream are equally delicious desserts.

To suggest that one idea, behavior, or choice is superior to another is to be labeled "intolerant" in our culture. Although pseudotolerance has a superficial resemblance to true tolerance, it is radically different from it in four ways:

## ★ Pseudotolerance Rejects the Idea of Absolute Truth ★

I realize *absolute truth* is one of those terms that is often thrown around in conversation without an understanding of what it really means. Absolute truth refers to that which is true regardless of context. For example, the statement that "7 x 8 = 56" is an absolute truth. There is no situation in which that assertion is not true. Regardless of a person's culture, country of origin, religious preference, or knowledge of the multiplication tables, 7 x 8 will always equal 56.

In contrast to absolute truths, there are relative truths. "Seventy-two degrees is the perfect temperature" is a relative truth. A person's gender, habitat, metabolism, clothing preference, and other variables may lead him to a different belief about the ideal setting for the thermostat. Obviously, everyone accepts the reality of relative truth, even when it comes to areas of morality.

For example, "We should obey the law" is not an absolute truth. There are some contexts in which most people would acknowledge that a person should disobey the law. For example, if you were rushing to the hospital at 2 a.m. with your child and you encountered a red light, most people would agree that it is permissible to run the red light if the intersection was clear. Even the Bible commands us to disobey government authorities when their laws contradict God's commands (Acts 5:29). While we should obey the law most of the time, there are some exceptions to that general principle.

However, proponents of pseudotolerance want to label the majority of moral and spiritual principles as "relative" rather than "absolute." The "Declarations of Principles on Tolerance," issued by the United Nations, encapsulates that principle with this simple and, ironically, absolute statement: "Tolerance . . . involves the rejection of dogmatism and absolutism."[15]

Those who embrace pseudotolerance find it almost impossible to label any act as "right" or "wrong." For example, were the terrorist attacks against our nation on September 11, 2001 evil? The relativist (one who rejects the concept of absolute truth) would answer, "It depends." From the perspective of the families of the nearly three thousand victims of that horrific day, the acts of those terrorists were wrong. However, that moral judgment is relative to the person's cultural context. Someone who lost a loved one would conclude those murders were wrong. But the relativist would argue that a person living in an oppressed Muslim country might believe the terrorists were courageous heroes for launching an attack against "The Great Satan" known as America. One Muslim imam in fact made such an assertion shortly after the terrorist attacks.

Pseudotolerance requires rejecting the belief that any moral or spiritual truths apply to all people regardless of their situation. Instead of saying, "Abortion is wrong," you can only say, "Abortion is wrong for me." Instead of judging homosexuality as a perversion, you can only say, "Homosexuality is not my choice." Instead of claiming that faith in Jesus Christ is the only way for anyone to experience heaven, you can only say, "Jesus Christ is the way to heaven for Christians." The late Christian philosopher Dr. Francis Schaeffer accurately summarized the result of rejecting absolute truth:

If there is no absolute moral standard, then one cannot say in a final sense that anything is right or wrong. By *absolute* we mean that which always applies, that which provides a final or ultimate standard. There must be an absolute if there are to be *morals*, and there must be an absolute if there are to be real *values*. If there is no absolute beyond man's ideas, then there is no final appeal to judge between individuals and groups whose moral judgments conflict. We are merely left with conflicting opinions.[16]

Ironically, the adherents of the new tolerance who vehemently reject the notion of absolute moral and spiritual truth must become what they say they despise, which leads to a second characteristic of the new tolerance.

## ★ Pseudotolerance Is Intolerant of Other Points of View ★

While he was editor of *Proceedings of the Biological Society of Washington*, Dr. Richard Sternberg received a submission for an article from Dr. Stephen Meyer of the Discovery Institute, an organization dedicated to the promotion of the intelligent design theory of the origins of the universe. Dr. Meyer's submission was titled "The Origin of Biological Information and the Higher Taxonomic Categories" (sounds like a real page-turner!). Sternberg and some of his peers decided to publish the article, which questioned Darwin's theories and made a case for an intelligent designer. Dr. Sternberg was immediately attacked by his peers for allowing the publication of the article. Members of the scientific community began a smear campaign against him, attempting to discredit him as a scientist simply because he published a paper from someone who did not toe the scientific party line about evolution.[17]

This incident is far from an isolated occurrence. In June 2006, the national science academies of sixty-seven countries warned parents and teachers about any attempts to undermine the teaching of evolution or allowing students to be taught that the world was created in six days.[18] In November 2007 the Parliamentary Assembly of the Council of Europe adopted a resolution that recommended a prohibition against the teaching of creationism in any educational setting outside of religion classes. The statement declared, "If we are not careful, creationism could become a threat to human rights."[19]

Several years ago I was invited to be a panelist for a symposium at the largest Jewish temple in Dallas concerning the principle of the separation of church and state in the public school system. On the panel with me was a Jewish rabbi, a minister from a liberal mainline denomination, and a member of the Texas State Board of Education. I was the token evangelical conservative. During the discussion, one of the panelists asked, "Dr. Jeffress, why are you so opposed to the teaching of evolution in the classroom?" I responded, "I'm not opposed at all to teaching the theory of evolution in the classroom. I want to know why you are so opposed to also allowing the alternative theory of creationism to be presented along with evolution as a possible explanation for the origin of life."

The truth is that the proponents of pseudotolerance are just as intolerant of ideas with which they disagree as the most rabid conservative. In fact, in some ways they are even more so because they argue for the suppression of ideas that contradict their own convictions. In January 2009, a sharply divided Texas State Board of Education voted to abandon a longtime requirement that high school science teachers discuss some of the weaknesses of the theory of evolution in biology classes. Proponents of this new policy argued that graduates of Texas high schools would be denied entrance into respected universities if they came from schools that allowed any questioning of Darwin's theory!

Doesn't scientific inquiry require the testing of theories and hypotheses? No respected biologist who believes in creationism or intelligent design would argue that the theory of evolution should not be taught in the classroom or discussed in scientific journals. Every proponent of creationism or intelligent design I know welcomes the questioning of his theory. Why are liberal educators so closed-minded to the point of paranoia about allowing full discussion of their theories?

Those who worship at the shrine of tolerance are often some of the most intolerant people, especially when it comes to the issue of "choice." Although the *Roe v. Wade* decision granted women the right to choose to kill their unborn children, one would imagine that medical professionals would be granted the right to choose not to murder an unborn child by refusing to participate in abortions. Fortunately, the federal government has in place a law known as the Weldon Amendment, protecting medical professionals from discrimination for their decision not to be involved in abortions. However, Planned Parenthood and the American Civil Liberties Union are challenging that law on the basis that a mother's right to choose to kill her child preempts the right of a doctor's choice not to kill the child![20]

The intolerance of the new pseudotolerance reaches into spiritual issues. Consider this statement from the Reverend Dr. William R. Murry, a prominent Unitarian Universalist minister and former president of Meadville/Lombard Theological School in Chicago:

I get a little impatient with the concept that we should tolerate all religions because people are entitled to their own beliefs. If a religion is based on ignorance and irrationality and totalitarianism, there is no need to stand aside and pretend that that's OK. What I would say about tolerance is that we cannot tolerate intolerance.[21]

"We cannot tolerate intolerance." That statement better than any other exposes the blatant hypocrisy of pseudotolerance.

## ★ Pseudotolerance Doesn't Differentiate Between People and Their Beliefs and Behaviors ★

Recently, I received this e-mail from a woman who had visited our church several times:

I grew up Catholic and went to sixteen years of Catholic school, met and dated a Protestant, and asked him to convert to Catholicism before we were married. We went on to have our children baptized in the Catholic faith. Several years ago we became inspired to attend _____ Baptist Church. From that day on, we have raised our children as Baptists. Not too long ago, in fact, our entire family was baptized at _____ church. We have attended your church a few times since we have moved to Dallas. We have felt very welcome at First Baptist and believe we could be more actively involved in First Baptist and perhaps join. We also have enjoyed your sermons, and particularly appreciate the firmness of your convictions. I have to say, though, that I was hurt by your implication, during your October 26 sermon, that Catholicism is a "false religion." My family members are devout Catholics and my own Catholic upbringing is still important to me. I personally believe you can be a faithful follower of Jesus Christ, without questioning the validity of other Christian denominations or suggesting they are "false religions." That is not a very welcoming message for those who are considering attending or joining First Baptist.

This woman's e-mail was in response to a message I had preached from Galatians 1:8 in which the apostle Paul condemns any "gospel" that teaches we are saved through faith and works rather than by God's grace alone. I claimed that many respectable Christian denominations and religions (including Catholicism) are proclaiming a false gospel, even though many within those denominations—including Catholicism—are believers. Although this woman claims to believe that salvation is through faith in Christ alone, she believes that criticism of any other belief system is "not a very welcoming message" to those of differing beliefs. Why?

She, along with many others, has become a victim of one of the basic tenets of pseudotolerance: you cannot separate people from their beliefs or behaviors. To reject Islam is to reject Muslims. If you oppose same-sex marriages, you must hate homosexuals. If you lobby for the repeal of *Roe. v. Wade*, then you must despise every woman who has ever had an abortion.

The result of equating people with their beliefs is the stifling of public discourse and even private conversations. If speaking out against certain ideas or behaviors is tantamount to hating the people who embrace those ideas or participate in those behaviors, who wants to be vilified as a hate-monger? For example, have you ever noticed how television programs and movies portray those who oppose homosexuality, support the choice of life over abortion, or embrace the belief that faith in Christ is the only way to be saved?

Usually they are portrayed as ignorant, bigoted, foaming-at-the-mouth fundamentalists who hate everything and everyone. For the average viewer, such a characterization results in an "I never want to be like that!" response. By equating the rejection of ideas and behavior with the hatred of people, the proponents of the new tolerance are effectively silencing debate and eliminating opposition to their agenda.

## ★ Embracing True Tolerance ★

For you and me to be the salt and light Jesus commanded us to be, we must reject every vestige of pseudotolerance. Salt must remain salty to be an effective preservative. Light must not be hidden to illuminate the darkness. If we buy into the concept that all moral choices are equally valid, we have no logical reason for opposing those behaviors that will hasten the destruction of our culture. If we subscribe to the idea that all paths ultimately lead to the same God, we have no basis for proclaiming that Jesus Christ is the only Light that will direct people toward heaven.

However, instead of rejecting the concept of tolerance altogether, I am convinced that Christians need to return to the historic (and more importantly, biblical) understanding of tolerance. Modeling what I call *true tolerance* can actually enhance our preserving influence on the culture and boost the brightness of our witness for Christ. How does true tolerance differ from pseudotolerance?

## ★ True Tolerance Requires Making a Judgment ★

Remember, you can only tolerate that with which you disagree (like same-sex marriages) or dislike (such as key lime pie). Disagreement and dislike are the result of making a judgment that some behaviors, choices, and ideas are superior to others. On a simplistic level, my decision to purchase a red tie instead of a blue one is built upon the judgment I made that one color looks better than the other. My choice of a mate required making a judgment about the superiority of my wife, Amy, over other potential choices. Life is filled with choices, and every choice requires a judgment.

Yet the proponents of pseudotolerance have convinced many people that it is unloving, unkind, and even un-Christian to make any kind of moral or spiritual judgments. Many times I have heard those who embrace pseudotolerance defend their distaste for labeling any behavior, choice, or idea as wrong by saying, "After all, Jesus said, 'Judge not lest you be judged.'"

Yet looking at Jesus' statement in its context provides a completely different perspective on the subject of making judgments:

> Do not judge so that you will not be judged. For in the way you judge, you will be judged; and by your standard of measure, it will be measured to you. Why do you look at the speck that is in your brother's eye, but do not notice the log that is in your own eye? Or how can you say to your brother, 'Let me take the speck out of your eye,' and behold, the log is in your own eye? You hypocrite, first take the log out of your own eye, and then you will see clearly to take the speck out of your brother's eye. (Matthew 7:1–5)

Jesus' words about judgment were directed toward the Pharisees, a religious sect known for holding people to a standard of behavior that the Pharisees were unwilling to live by themselves. Jesus warned about condemning the behavior of others in order to mask your own moral deficiencies. We all know of government and religious leaders who speak publicly about upholding family values while privately engaging in the same immorality they condemn.

It is obvious from Jesus' words that He is not opposed to every kind of judgment. For example, Jesus said if you encounter someone with a particle of dust or sliver of wood in his eye, you should try to remove it from his eye. Just make sure, Jesus warned, that your vision is not impaired so you might see clearly to perform the procedure safely. Would you want a blindfolded ophthalmologist working on your eye (or as Jesus described it, one with a wooden plank protruding from his own eye)? The reminder to remove obstructions from your own eye before you operate on your neighbor's eye is not a command not to touch your neighbor's eye at all, but to do so carefully.

The compassionate decision to help your neighbor remove the speck from his eye requires making a number of judgments:

- Specks do not belong in the human eye.
- Specks are uncomfortable.
- Discomfort is bad.
- We are morally obligated to alleviate discomfort in others.

Obviously, Jesus had more in mind here than helping people maintain clear vision. Whenever we see someone living apart from God's standards (and experiencing the resulting pain of doing so), we should do everything in our power to help him rather than condemn him. But before we can help anyone deal with sin in his life, we need to make sure we have confronted sin in our own life. Identifying and removing sin in others and ourselves requires making a series of judgments:

- There is a God to whom I am accountable.
- God's expectations for my life are revealed in His Word.
- This behavior is a sin because it is contrary to God's Word.
- Sin is ultimately harmful, not helpful.

Jesus' analogy about the right way to judge other people leads to a second characteristic of true tolerance.

## ★ True Tolerance Is Grounded in a Genuine Concern for Others ★

The only reason for helping someone remove a particle from his eye is a desire for the well-being of that individual. Yes, the procedure requires making the judgment that there is something wrong with the person's eye. The effort to remove the particle may actually result in some temporary discomfort for the other person. But the motivation for making the judgment and inflicting the pain is the long-term comfort of the other person.

The proponents of pseudotolerance have successfully ingrained in the populace the idea that labeling any behavior or ideas as "wrong" is unloving and even hateful. But demonstrating tolerance toward other people or cultures does not require our refraining from making judgments about their behavior, ideas, or choices. In fact, remaining silent about behavior, ideas, or choices that will ultimately bring harm to an individual (or nation) demonstrates a lack of love for other people.

The apostle Paul criticized the Christians at the church in Corinth for their unwillingness to confront a member who was involved in an illicit sexual relationship:

You have become arrogant and have not mourned instead, so that the one who had done this deed would be removed from your midst. (1 Corinthians 5:2)

Perhaps the church leaders in Corinth prided themselves in the fact that they were an accepting, grace-filled, tolerant church that did not judge other people. But their acceptance of such immorality in their congregation was proof of their indifference toward the well-being of both the sinning individual and the church. Paul demanded that they remove the unrepentant man from their congregation "so that his spirit may be saved in the day of the Lord Jesus" (1 Corinthians 5:5). Suffering the embarrassment of public exposure and removal from the church would certainly be temporarily painful for this man— but not nearly as painful as facing the ultimate judgment of God.

Don't fall for the mistaken belief that making judgments about another person's behavior or beliefs is hateful. The famous evangelist of yesteryear, Charles Finney, once remarked, "If you see your neighbor sin and you pass by and neglect to reprove him, it is just as cruel as if you should see his house on fire, and pass by and not warn him of it."[22] Genuinely caring about another person sometimes requires that we confront that person about wrong behaviors or beliefs.

## ★ True Tolerance Allows for Preferences ★

Proponents of pseudotolerance have convinced the public that tolerance necessitates neutrality. "To be truly accepting of others we must never express our own feelings about issues," we are told. Let me illustrate what I mean.

Recently, I became concerned about the growing trend among businesses and organizations of refusing to acknowledge Christmas. We have all seen and read reports of businesses that instructed their employees to say "Happy Holidays" rather than "Merry Christmas." In my city, a local bank removed a Christmas tree from its lobby because some customers were offended by the tree! I decided that I wanted to do something positive to stem the tide of secularism that is sweeping our county, so our church established a website called Grinchalert.com. We encouraged people around the country to go to our website and place businesses that shun Christmas on the "naughty list" and place businesses that acknowledge Christmas on the "nice list."

As you might imagine, the website received a lot of national attention. Hundreds of thousands of people visited the website after CNN, Fox News, and other media outlets reported the story. One reporter asked me, "What about a Jewish person who owns a plumbing business who chooses not to acknowledge Christmas?" I responded, "That is perfectly fine. We live in a pluralistic society in which everyone is free to make his own choices and then live with the consequences of those choices."

I am not offended by seeing a Jewish menorah at Christmas or having someone say "Happy Hanukkah" rather than "Merry Christmas." True tolerance demands that I accept a person's choice not to celebrate Christmas. However, true tolerance also allows me not only the right to say "Merry Christmas" but to try to persuade individuals and organizations to acknowledge the uniqueness of this holiday.

From the perspective of government, true tolerance demands that we allow people to embrace beliefs with which we disagree and to engage in behaviors we might find objectionable within the boundaries of established law. However, the fact that our Constitution demands that everyone have the freedom to embrace any religious beliefs (or no religious beliefs) does not mean that the government cannot demonstrate a preference for Christianity. Many people erroneously believe that the First Amendment of the Constitution demands governmental neutrality or even hostility toward Christianity:

> Congress shall make no law respecting an establishment of religion or prohibiting the free exercise thereof . . .

In recent years this so-called establishment clause has been used to ban nativity scenes from public property and prohibit prayers at graduation ceremonies because such outward religious expressions imply the government's endorsement of a specific religion. The problem with such an application of the First Amendment is that it is based on a misunderstanding of the words "religion" and "establishment." The First Amendment was meant to guarantee that no particular denomination *within Christianity* would be elevated above other denominations to become a national church in which all citizens would be forced to worship. How do we know that?

Supreme Court Justice Joseph Story was appointed to the Court by President James Madison in 1811. Since President Madison was considered the chief author and father of the Constitution, he would only nominate to the High Court someone who understood and shared his understanding of the Constitution. How did Joseph Story interpret the First Amendment? In his commentaries on the Constitution of the United States, Story clarified the meaning of the First Amendment and its implication for religious toleration, and specifically, the religion of Islam:

The real object of the [First] Amendment was not to countenance, much less to advance Mahometanism [Islam], or Judaism, or infidelity by prostrating Christianity; but to exclude all rivalry among Christian sects and to prevent any national ecclesiastical establishment which should give to a hierarchy the exclusive patronage of the national government.[23]

Justice Story understood the word *religion* in the First Amendment to be a synonym for "Christian denominations" rather than for other faiths such as Islam or Judaism. Although the Constitution allows people to embrace and practice other faiths, the granting of that right is in no way to be construed as an admission that such religions are as equally valid as Christianity. As New York State Supreme Court chief justice James Kent wrote in the case of *The People v. Ruggles* (1811):

... we are a Christian people, and the morality of the country is deeply engrafted upon Christianity, and not upon the doctrines or worship of those impost[e]rs.[24]

The framers of the Constitution and the earliest American jurists demonstrated a clear preference for Christianity. They did not hesitate to declare that America was a Christian nation. John Jay, the first chief justice of the Supreme Court, referred to America as "our Christian nation."[25] Although these jurists championed the right of citizens to choose other faiths, that right did not demand that government engage in what Joseph Story called "prostrating Christianity."

There is no mandate in the Constitution that requires the government to prohibit expressions of the Christian faith in the public square. In fact, as I have demonstrated in several examples, the

First Amendment does not even require that the government treat all faiths equally. Although the Constitution demands that the government allow expressions of all faiths, the government can (and for more than 150 years did) show a preference for the Christian faith. A high school principal does not have to have both a Christian and a Muslim student offer a prayer at graduation. A city mayor is not obligated to balance a nativity scene in the town square with a Jewish menorah. True tolerance allows for preferences by individuals.

Recently I was interviewed by one of the few liberals at Fox News, Alan Colmes. Alan went on a diatribe about my belief that Christianity offered the only true way to God. He accused me of being "hateful" toward people of different faiths because I had suggested in a forum for religious writers in Washington D.C. that Christians should give preference to voting for Christians. "So, you want to keep Jews, Muslims, and Hindus from running for office?" Colmes asked. "I didn't say that," I responded. "I said that Christians have every right to prefer to vote for Christians over non-Christians." The talk show host never grasped how someone could tolerate different perspectives than his own and yet show a preference for one definitive viewpoint. Colmes is a victim of pseudotolerance.

Yet whenever we demonstrate our preference for life over abortion, heterosexuality over homosexuality, Christianity over other faiths, we need to follow the example of Jesus Christ. Those who picture Jesus as a mild-mannered, milquetoast guy who roamed the Judean countryside picking sunflowers and eating birdseed don't know the Jesus of the Bible. This guy could be really tough when it came to some of His statements:

Do not think that I came to bring peace on the earth; I did not come to bring peace, but a sword. (Matthew 10:34)

If your hand causes you to stumble, cut it off; it is better for you to end life crippled, than, having your two hands, to go into hell, into the unquenchable fire. (Mark 9:43)

If anyone comes to Me, and does not hate his own father and mother and wife and children and brothers and sisters, yes, and even his own life, he cannot be My disciple. (Luke 14:26)

Jesus had an uncanny knack for being able to be tough with His beliefs but tender toward people (except for those religious hypocrites, the Pharisees). Jesus Christ is a perfect example of what I call a "velvet-covered brick." If we are ever going to influence our culture by influencing the individuals who comprise our culture, we have to demonstrate that same balance between conviction and compassion.

Yet compassion doesn't negate conviction. True tolerance not only allows for a strong point of view; it demands it. True tolerance is based upon a genuine concern for people who embrace beliefs and practice behaviors that will ultimately bring them harm. True tolerance says, "I respect your right to believe as you do, but I care too much about you to remain silent." William Watkins in his book *The New Absolutes* writes,

We must violate the new tolerance and become people marked by intolerance. Not an intolerance that unleashes hate upon people, but an intolerance that's unwilling to allow error to masquerade as truth. An intolerance that calls evil *evil*, and good *good*.[26]

To be the salt and light requires us to risk being labeled intolerant by those who have distorted true tolerance. The most effective way we can "violate the new tolerance" and stem the tide of evil that is about to destroy our country is the subject of the next chapter.

# CHAPTER
## 4

## How a Christian Should Vote

**P**olitics. The word alone can produce a bitter aftertaste. The word and its derivations are almost always used in a pejorative sense. For example, the observation "That's just politics" implies that a particular issue is of secondary rather than primary importance. The charge hurled at pastors and churches who are "getting too involved in politics" suggests that they are forfeiting their primary calling for activities that have no relationship with the kingdom of God. And woe to the person who chooses to make "politics" his life calling! Used car salesmen, televangelists, and drug dealers enjoy more respect than someone who carries the label of "politician."

It is easy to see why politics is treated with disdain by so many. The mudslinging that accompanies every election, the pandering to special interest groups, and the tendency to allow policy to be shaped by poll numbers rather than deeply held convictions make politics and politicians suspect. Such realities also cause Christians to question whether they should individually and corporately allow themselves to be tainted by such a tawdry business.

However, in its purest form politics is the art or science of government. To say that Christians should not be involved in politics is to say that believers should not have anything to do with government. The argument is that since our "citizenship is in heaven" (Philippians 3:20) and we are "aliens and strangers" in this world (1 Peter 2:11), Christians should leave the business of governing to unbelievers. After all, since everything in this world will one day be destroyed by fire and the kingdoms of this world will eventually be replaced with the kingdom of God, why invest any time and effort in trying to influence that which is transitory at best?

The simple answer is that in commanding us to be "salt" in the world, Jesus is encouraging us to influence our culture rather than isolate ourselves from our culture. Granted, we will not be able to reverse the decay and prevent the destruction of the world as we know it, but through our efforts we can stall the rotting process. However, influencing our culture requires contact with our culture.

In the previous chapter I described our church's website encouraging businesses and organizations to acknowledge Christmas as a religious holiday by saying, "Merry Christmas" rather than the politically correct "Happy holidays." Apparently, the website struck a nerve with the country. We heard the predictable outcries from secularists and liberals, accusing us of trying to "bully" non-Christians into worshipping God. But I was surprised by the negative reaction of some conservative Christians who denounced our efforts as "un-loving," "intolerant," and "misdirected." After probing deeper with these critics, I discovered that they believed that Christians had no business trying to change their culture. Trying to alter the behavior of non-Christians was both brutal and futile, I was told.

The wide coverage our efforts received in the national media, along with some of the scathing columns and letters to the editor in our local newspaper, raised questions in the minds of some of our members about the wisdom of what appeared to be a no-brainer issue. At the end of our church services one Sunday I explained to our congregation and the larger media audience my rationale in what I thought was a fun way to make a serious point.

"I would put this effort in the same category as striving to keep 'In God We Trust' on our coins, allowing prayers at government meetings, and posting the Ten Commandments in courtrooms," I said. "I realize none of these actions will ever get anyone into heaven. But I believe our country is healthier when there is at least a public acknowledgment of God than it will be if we allow the secularists to remove any mention of God from the public sector. I realize not everyone agrees, but I'm not willing to wave the white flag and sur-render our country to the atheists and secularists." The congregation responded with a standing ovation, but not everyone was convinced.

No one wanted to be outed as a Grinch by opposing their pas-tor on the centrality of Christmas, but people still harbored ques-tions about the propriety of Christians trying to influence—even in-directly through a "Grinch list"—the behavior of unbelievers. Since the word *govern* means to control, direct, or influence the actions of others, this issue goes beyond simply creating "naughty" and "nice" lists at Christmas. The fundamental question is, "What role should Christians play in government?"

Those who argue that Christians have no business trying to influence the actions of others, especially unbelievers, are answering, "None." As one television anchor said to me in an interview, "I'm a Christian and believe that Christ is central to Christmas. But I have no right to try to force my belief on others." Encouraging organizations to acknowledge Christmas hardly seems akin to holding a sword over someone's head and threatening, "Worship Jesus or die!"

However, the presupposition behind the television anchor's exaggerated characterization of my efforts is that to exert *any* pressure on the behavior of non-Christians is wrong. Some might concede that it is permissible to influence an unbeliever to trust in Christ, but they would argue that anything beyond that is out of bounds. Therefore, the argument continues, Christians should not try to influence non-Christians by involving themselves in politics (the art of governing). After all, government by definition is the act of controlling the behavior of citizens.

How have Christians arrived at this conclusion? Many believers have embraced a compartmentalized view of Christianity that demands they keep their faith in a spiritual silo. You may embrace whatever faith you choose. You might even want to (gently) persuade someone else to adopt your religious convictions. But you must never use your spiritual beliefs to affect the behavior of society. The late philosopher Francis Schaeffer highlighted the fallacy of such reasoning:

> A platonic concept of spirituality which does not include all of life is not true biblical spirituality. True spirituality touches all of life, including things of government and law, and not just "religious things."[1]

Jesus Christ is Lord, not just over Christians, but over everyone. Although His complete and uncontested reign over the earth will be experienced in the future (a time many Christians refer to as the Millennium), He still exerts control over the world today. We understand that as the Head of the church, Christ directs the activities of all believers. But God also exerts influence over non-Christians in the world today through government.

Consider Paul's instructions to the Christians living under the rule of the emperor Nero. It would have been understandable for Paul to try to distance God from any connection with Nero's evil empire. Instead, Paul reminds believers that government is an arm of God's rule over humanity:

> Every person is to be in subjection to the governing authorities. For there is no authority except from God, and those which exist are established by God. Therefore whoever resists authority has opposed the ordinance of God; and they who have opposed will receive condemnation upon themselves. (Romans 13:1–2)

This passage is not an absolute prohibition against defying government under any circumstance but a warning against the mindset of many Christians today that divorces God from government. During the reign of Christ upon the earth, God will place His Son on the throne of David in Jerusalem to enact His policies of justice and righteousness over all the earth. But God also uses the governing authorities today to execute His will:

> For rulers are not a cause of fear for good behavior, but for evil. Do you want to have no fear of authority? Do what is good and you will have praise from the same; for it is a minister of God

to you for good. But if you do what is evil, be afraid; for it does not bear the sword for nothing; for it is a minister of God, an avenger who brings wrath on the one who practices evil. (Romans 13:3–4)

If government is an extension of God's rule over the world today, then it is logical to conclude that God must be involved in the process of selecting governing officials. Scripture assures us that He is.

Paul says that governing officials "are established by God" (Romans 13:1). Even the prophet Daniel, who had several run-ins with ungodly rulers, recognized that God is ultimately the One who "removes kings and establishes kings" (Daniel 2:21). Wouldn't it be nice if God would spare us from all the political campaigns that are accompanied by endless chatter and speculation in the media? God could just fill every governmental vacancy each year with His slate of candidates.

But God is subtler than that. He usually chooses to work through the human processes in place to select the governing authorities. In some cultures, a leader inherits his right to rule through a monarchy. In other situations, family dynasties select from among themselves those who will control a nation. But as John Jay, America's first chief justice of the Supreme Court wrote, "Providence [God] has given to our people the choice of their rulers."[2]

Since our nation allows its citizens to select their leaders (who are an extension of God's rule), should not God's people be instrumental in influencing the selection of those leaders? After all, *some* set of values is going to govern or control a nation. Those values will be determined—or at least shaped—by the leaders of that nation. Why shouldn't Christians work to select leaders who will govern a nation according to God's principles?

## ★ Once Upon a Time ★

Travel back with me twenty-six hundred years to Judah, the Southern Kingdom of Israel. The king of your country has just died. He was an evil ruler who, like his father, led the nation into idolatry, witchcraft, and child sacrifices to pagan deities. Now that the king is dead, you receive word that you have been chosen as the new monarch of the nation.

Do you think God would care whether you followed in the footsteps of your father and grandfather? Suppose a reporter from the *Jerusalem Times* asked you how your faith would impact your policies as king, and you responded, "Well, I personally believe in Jehovah God, but I don't have the right to impose my personal beliefs on the nation. If people want to worship other gods and sacrifice innocent children, that it is their right." Do you imagine God would be pleased by your determination to separate your personal beliefs from your public responsibility?

The scenario I just described actually occurred in the seventh century BC. King Amon and his father, Manasseh, had been the most evil kings to date in Judah's history. After Amon's death, Josiah became king at the ripe old age of eight! But instead of following in his father's and grandfather's footsteps, Josiah charted a new direction for the nation. He destroyed the places of pagan worship, repaired the temple, forbade the practices of witchcraft and child sacrifice, and led the nation in a great national revival. The result? God granted Josiah His divine seal of approval:

Before him [Josiah] there was no king like him who turned to the LORD with all his heart and with all his soul and with all his might, according to all the law of Moses; nor did any like him arise after him. However, the LORD did not turn from the fierceness of His great wrath with which his anger burned against Judah, because of all the provocations with which Manasseh had provoked Him. (2 Kings 23:25–26)

King Josiah was not able to reverse the spiritual decay of Judah and spare the nation from God's inevitable judgment. However, he was able to buy a little more time for his country by enacting policies based on God's righteousness rather than popular consensus.

You and I will never be installed as "king of America." However, unlike Judah and other monarchies, we are the leaders of our country because our government is "of the people, by the people, and for the people."[3] King Josiah had a choice to make. He could continue the ungodly policies of his father and grandfather, or he could govern his nation according to God's holy principles. Obviously, God had a definite opinion about how Josiah should lead!

In our country, we are the ones who have been given the privilege of selecting our leaders who, in turn, will determine the direction of our nation. Given what Scripture reveals about the character of God, do you think He cares whether our leaders promote the killing of the unborn, embrace sexual immorality, or encourage the worship of other gods? Has God's nature changed during the last three thousand years, making Him more "inclusive" and "tolerant" of other viewpoints?

Just as Josiah determined the spiritual and moral direction of his nation by the policies he enacted, you and I cast our vote for righteousness or unrighteousness by the leaders we elect. To suggest that Christians should not be involved in politics is to imply that God really does not care about the spiritual direction of our country. Given God's past dealings with other nations, can anyone seriously believe that?

Some leader will be elected to every office and bring with him a core set of beliefs that will shape his decisions and, therefore, the direction of the nation. It only makes sense that Christians should be at the forefront of selecting leaders who embrace principles and formulate policies that are more likely to bring God's favor rather than His wrath upon our country.

## ★ How to Select a Candidate ★

In a representative government like that of the United States, our leaders serve as our proxy. Hopefully, if elected, our candidates will make the decisions we would make if we were in their place. Yet most of us have had the experience of voting for a candidate who disappointed us once elected. After the election of President George W. Bush to a second term, I remember participating in a number of conference calls with conservatives who were privately disappointed in the president's lack of willingness to enact policies he had championed while running for office. Likewise, many liberals openly voice displeasure with President Barack Obama for taking a more centrist position on some issues as he prepares to run for reelection in 2012.

For Christians who are selecting a candidate, let me suggest four criteria that may not eliminate but can lessen the possibility of voters' remorse. The answers to these four questions will help you determine whether a candidate is likely to vote for righteousness or unrighteousness once elected.

## ★ Question #1: Is the Candidate a Christian? ★

Being a Christian does not automatically qualify someone for office. In my opinion some of the weakest presidents we have had were men who claimed to be born-again believers, including two who were Southern Baptists. However, if given a choice between a competent Christian and non-Christian, voting for a Christian candidate is preferable. Earlier I quoted John Jay, the first chief justice of the United States Supreme Court, who wrote about the unique privilege God has given us to select our leaders. Jay was unapologetic in suggesting what kind of candidate Christians should prefer:

> Providence has given to our people the choice of their rulers, and it is the duty, as well as the privilege and interest of our Christian nation to select and prefer Christians for their rulers.[4]

As a coauthor of the Federalist Papers and respected jurist, Chief Justice John Jay was intimately acquainted with Article VI of the United States Constitution, which had been ratified only a few years before Jay made this statement in a private letter to Jedidiah Morse. The Constitution is clear that "no religious test shall ever be required as a qualification to any office or public trust under the United States." Many times I have had opponents in a debate (even conservatives) label the idea of preferring Christians over non-Christians as "unconstitutional" according to Article VI. However, Jay clearly understood that while government could not impose religious tests for candidates, individuals could and should consider a candidate's spiritual convictions as a criterion for suitability for office.

Why should we prefer Christian over non-Christian leaders? A Christian leader is more likely to enact godly principles than a non-

Christian. A non-Christian is certainly capable of embracing biblical values. For example, there are non-Christian politicians who oppose abortion and support heterosexual marriage for any number of reasons. Perhaps they do so for political expediency or because of the influence of a friend or parent.

But such convictions can quickly change unless they are grounded in a person's deeper beliefs about God. However, if an elected official really believes that he is accountable to God for the decisions he makes, he is less likely to allow external pressure to alter his beliefs. As the writer of Proverbs says, "The fear of the LORD is the beginning of knowledge" (Proverbs 1:7).

The value of electing Christian leaders is not limited to the policies he enacts. Christian politicians have the advantage of experiencing God's leadership in making crucial decisions. For example, one of the most difficult decisions any president confronts is the decision to go to war against another nation. Such a decision not only affects the military personnel directly involved in the conflict, but it can impact the survival of the entire nation.

Suppose a hostile nation is threatening the security of our country. Would you prefer a president who only looked within himself and to his advisers for guidance? Or would you feel more secure with a president who sought the best counsel of others but also looked to God for direction? Only Christians can claim the leading of God in making important decisions. "For all who are being led by the Spirit of God, these are sons of God" (Romans 8:14).

Christian leaders (with some very notable exceptions) are also more likely to demonstrate the integrity of character that voters generally desire. Their core beliefs serve as a restraint against immorality, corruption, and dereliction of duty. It is popular to argue that a politician's personal life has no impact on his public service.

Billionaire Ross Perot, who ran as a third-party presidential candidate in 1992, highlighted the absurdity of that argument when he pointed out that if a man was willing to lie to his own wife about an affair, why would he not lie to the country he served? Nearly two hundred years earlier Noah Webster, the lexicographer and man known as the father of American scholarship and education, wrote:

In selecting men for office, let principle be your guide. Regard not the particular sect or denomination of the candidate—look to his character. It is alleged by men of loose principles, or defective views of the subject, that religion and morality are not necessary or important qualifications for political stations. But the Scriptures teach a different doctrine. They direct that rulers should be men "who rule in the fear of God, able men, such as fear God, men of truth, hating covetousness" [Exodus 18:21]. . . . [I]t is to the neglect of this rule of conduct in our citizens, that we must ascribe the multiplied frauds, breaches of trust, peculations [white-collar larceny] and embezzlements of public property which astonish even ourselves; which tarnish the character of our country; which disgrace a republican government.[5]

Although the Constitution prohibits the government from imposing a religious litmus test for candidates seeking office, no such restriction applies to individual citizens. In fact, Christians who refuse to consider a candidate's spiritual qualifications are acting irresponsibly, according to John Witherspoon, one of the signers of the Declaration of Independence:

Those, therefore, who pay no regard to religion and sobriety in the persons whom they send to the legislature of any State are guilty of the greatest absurdity and will soon pay dear for their folly.[6]

Finally, Christian leaders who uphold godly principles enjoy the unique favor of God upon their lives. The Old Testament vividly contrasts those rulers with whom God was pleased and those kings who "did evil in the sight of the Lord." God's favor or disfavor of leaders spills over to the citizens as well. As the writer of Proverbs observes, "When the righteous increase, the people rejoice, but when a wicked man rules, people groan" (Proverbs 29:2).

Some people reject any comparison of Israel's history to our country today on the basis that Israel was a theocracy rather than a democracy like America. Although that is a valid observation, it is ultimately an irrelevant one if you believe in God's immutability. Although nations may change their preferred form of government, God never alters His immutable convictions. As the psalmist exclaimed, "Blessed is the nation whose God is the Lord" (Psalm 33:12). God will always favor a nation that is built on His timeless principles rather than one built on the shifting sands of public opinion.

But what if your choice comes down to voting for a qualified non-Christian or an unqualified Christian? Doesn't competency trump spirituality? Some people quote an alleged comment by Martin Luther: "I'd rather be ruled by a competent Turk than an incompetent believer." Such a declaration appears to make good sense, until you consider some obvious flaws in such an argument.

First, competency is a very subjective criterion. For example, what better qualifies someone to be president of the United States: experience in the business world or experience in governmental positions? Is a United States senator or a state governor better equipped to lead the nation? Many past occupants of the White House have noted that nothing can prepare a person for the unique challenges of sitting in the Oval Office. Ultimately it is a person's character—his morality, tenacity, diligence, and concern for others—that will determine his success or failure.

Second, to rise to become a political party's nominee for office (especially the presidency) requires a basic level of competency. Although I have vehemently disagreed with the policies of those I have voted against in past years, I cannot think of one candidate for a major office that I would label as "incompetent." Truthfully, I have been surprised by some candidates I thought were imminently qualified to serve who, after installed in office, proved otherwise.

Finally, Christians should work to ensure that we don't have to make such choices by encouraging competent believers to seek public office. A few years ago a member of our church, Tom Leppert, served as the CEO of the largest construction company in America. He was financially secure and could have remained in that position for as long as he wanted. Instead, he felt God calling him into politics. He gave up his lucrative career in the business world to become the mayor of Dallas, Texas. He began his term as mayor by reinstating prayers at city council meetings. He unashamedly claims to be a follower of Jesus Christ in public forums. Even unbelievers in our city hold him in high regard because of his superb leadership skills that have revitalized the city of Dallas and brought warring factions in city government together. He is now running for United States senator. Why? Tom feels that God has called him to be a politician as strongly as I feel that God has called me to be a pastor.

No one should be surprised that God would call some believers to serve in government. Throughout the Old Testament you see God appointing men and women to serve in places of influence to accomplish His purposes. Joseph became the manager of Potiphar's household and ultimately Pharaoh's right-hand man. God selected Esther to become the queen of Persia so that she could save His people. Daniel served as an adviser to two kings and was appointed one of three commissioners overseeing Babylon under King Darius.

God's interests in His world clearly extend beyond religious people and religious institutions and religious people. He reigns over all of the earth:

The LORD has established His throne in the heavens, and His sovereignty rules over all. (Psalm 103:19)

If God's rule encompasses all of the earth, then it only makes sense that He would call competent men and women to serve as extensions of His government over the world He controls.

## ★ How Can You Know? ★

An even more fundamental question that arises from using candidates' faith as a standard for voting is, "How do you really know if the candidate is a believer?" After all, in our culture asking someone, "Are you a Christian?" is almost tantamount to asking, "Are you an American?" The only candidates—especially those running for high office—who would not profess to be Christians would be those who embrace Judaism (which many link with Christianity) and Muslims (who for the sake of political correctness receive an automatic exemption). Most pseudo-Christian candidates are not trying to mislead the electorate in claiming to be believers. They sincerely believe that their commitment to being a good person qualifies them as followers of Jesus Christ.

So how can we know for sure whether a candidate is a genuine follower of Christ? Obviously, we can't know for sure about anyone's spiritual condition. However, choosing a candidate requires that we make a judgment about that person's relationship with Christ. One way to attempt an accurate assessment of a candidate's faith is through the words he uses to describe his conversion experience. A candidate who claims to have been a Christian "since the day I was born" or says he is "doing the best I can to get to heaven one day" obviously has no understanding of what Jesus meant when He said, " . . . unless one is born again he cannot see the kingdom of God" (John 3:3). Although the vocabulary chosen may vary among people, every genuine Christian should be able to articulate his faith in Christ's death on the cross for the forgiveness of sins.

However, a profession of faith is not enough to ensure that someone is an authentic believer. After all, Jesus also said that not everyone who calls Him "Lord" will be welcomed into heaven (Matthew 7:21–23). Beyond a person's words, we must also consider his works. Jesus inseparably linked belief and obedience when he said, "He who believes in the Son has eternal life; but he who does not obey the Son will not see life, but the wrath of God abides on him" (John 3:36). A candidate who claims to be a disciple of Christ but espouses beliefs and enacts policies that are contrary to the teachings of Christ is highly suspect.

For example, suppose I said that I was a follower of Charles Darwin, the father of evolution. But instead of accepting my claim at face value, you decided to probe a little deeper about my beliefs concerning the origin of life. In response to your questions, I answered, "Oh, I believe that God created the world in six days. I also believe that He formed Adam and Eve out of the dust of the earth rather than through a long process of small changes over billions of years." You would rightly conclude, "I don't care what you claim; you are not a follower of Charles Darwin! Your beliefs are contradictory to his most basic teachings."

Similarly, candidates who claim to be followers of Christ but espouse positions that are contrary to the teachings of Christ should be viewed skeptically. I realize that this is a highly subjective criterion (for example, are Jesus' words about treatment of the poor just as important as His words regarding marriage being reserved for a man and a woman?), but it is one that still needs to be considered.

The issue of preferring a Christian over a non-Christian candidate is especially explosive when it involves popular religions such as Mormonism. Historically, conservative theologians have treated Mormonism as a cult rather than a legitimate sect of Christianity. However, would a Mormon who opposes abortion and supports traditional values make a better candidate than someone who claims to be a Christian but embraces unbiblical positions? This question is likely to come to the forefront of discussion soon.

Former Utah governor Mitt Romney, a Mormon and political conservative, sought the Republican nomination in 2008 and is continuing his quest for president in 2012. During the 2008 election I was invited to participate in a debate in Washington D.C. with Christian attorney Jay Sekulow before the Religion Newswriters Association on the topic "Just How Christian Does a Presidential Candidate Need to Be?" Sekulow, a supporter of Governor Romney's 2008 presidential bid, claimed that the values of the candidate, not his theology, should be most important to Christian voters.

I reiterated a statement I made in our pulpit months earlier that had made national headlines and brought a flood of angry letters and e-mails from Salt Lake City: "Mitt Romney may make a wonderful president, but if you choose to vote for him, don't be under the illusion you are voting for a Christian. Mormonism is not Christianity. It is a false religion." I continued by pointing out the hypocrisy of evangelical leaders who had lectured the nation about the importance of having a Christian president during the eight years of the Bush administration, but now were saying there was no problem in electing a Mormon. As one evangelical leader who supported Romney said, "We are not electing a theologian-in-chief, but a commander-in-chief." Such a sudden change in position could cause voter whiplash. We must decide whether a candidate's religious faith matters. I closed my address to the religion writers with these words:

> Adherents of Mormonism, Islam, and Hinduism are not just worshipping our God in a different way. They are followers of false gods. In the Old Testament, God condemned any ruler who introduced the worship of other gods into national life. I think before a Christian could vote for someone who embraced a false religion such as Mormonism, he would need to carefully consider the eternal consequences that electing such a leader could have in legitimizing a false religion and, therefore, endangering the eternal destinies of those who might choose that leader's religion.

> Some strident evangelicals would counter, "But Robert, we could be talking about protecting the life of the unborn. Surely a candidate's position on abortion is more important than the religious faith he personally embraces." While I believe that protecting the physical life of the unborn is important, I believe that protecting the eternal life of those already born is also crucial. Admittedly, this is a unique Christian perspective, but Christians need to remember that our concern is not only with the well-

being of people in this life, but also in the life to come. Am I saying that under no circumstances should a Christian vote for an unbeliever, or even the follower of a false religion? No, but I am saying that in a contest between two candidates whose views on biblical issues are similar, a follower of Christ should always give preference to the Christian candidate.[7]

The response to my above comments is best described by a headline in the *Washington Times* a few days later: "Secular Scribes Stunned." The columnist noted, "I could see some of the scribes practically hyperventilating as the pastor talked. I could hear muttered comments. 'The nerve!' 'How dare he?' 'Where did they find this guy?' . . . One of the lunch organizers later said a lot of reporters were 'uncomfortable' with Mr. Jeffress' talk."[8]

Using a candidate's religious faith as a criterion for selection will never be popular in our country. The general electorate's ignorance of the Constitution, especially Article VI and the First Amendment, has led to the widely held assumption that mixing religion and politics is illegal and as potentially dangerous as combining two explosive chemicals. But as we have seen, history and, more importantly, Scripture teach us that consideration of a candidate's faith is not only permissible, but it is essential.

## ★ Question #2: How Would a Candidate's Faith Impact His Policies? ★

The 2004 presidential election involved two candidates from two political parties with two very different views of how faith should impact policy. Senator John Kerry, the Democratic Party nominee, said in an interview, "I fully intend to practice my religion as separate from what I do with respect to my public life."[9]

However, not everyone was willing to grant Senator Kerry the luxury of compartmentalizing his faith. A number of Catholic leaders condemned Kerry for his pro-abortion policies. While Kerry was campaigning in Missouri in February 2004, St. Louis archbishop Raymond Burke caused a national firestorm of controversy by forbidding Kerry from taking Communion while in the area because of the candidate's stand on abortion and stem cell research.

The Republican presidential candidate in 2004, President George W. Bush, had a different view of the integration of faith and policy. "You can't separate your faith from your life. . . . I don't see how you can separate your faith as a person, and my faith is an important part of my life," Bush told CNN interviewer Larry King on August 12, 2004.[10] President Bush's personal beliefs about abortion, same-sex marriage, and human rights—all of which where grounded in his religious faith—impacted his policies and judicial appointments.

Frankly, any politician who claims to be a Christian but claims that his Christianity has no influence on his public policies is either a dishonest politician or a shallow believer. The Bible teaches that a Christian's faith should impact every area of his life—his marriage, his finances, his friendships, and his career. How would you respond to someone who said, "I'm a Christian, but I keep my faith separate from my decisions about sex"? Such a thought is beyond ludicrous! God's Word encourages us:

Trust in the LORD with all your heart and do not lean on your own understanding. *In all your ways acknowledge Him*, and He will make your paths straight. (Proverbs 3:5–6; emphasis added)

Policy is not implemented in a vacuum. Every political leader has a core set of values that determine which policies he champions. Some leaders make decisions based on political expediency. Is this position popular with the constituents who elected them? Others are motivated by the quest for higher office. How will their vote play with the kingmakers in their party? Some politicians' values are shaped by their personal experiences. Growing up in an impoverished family makes some leaders more prone to enact laws that provide generous aid to the poor.

Every politician bases his decisions on his values. The real question is, what determines the politician's core set of values from which he determines his policies? Are his values shaped by political peers, popularity, ego, or by the unchanging principles of God's Word? Every political leader in the Bible who enjoyed God's favor was one who integrated his personal faith with his public life rather than segregating the two.

## ★ Question#3: Do His Policies Align with the Bible? ★

If we accept that the preferred candidate for office is one who shapes his policies according to Scripture, then it is important to measure his views by the standard of God's Word. Obviously, the Bible does not address the majority of issues that politicians must confront. To try to extrapolate from Scripture a "biblical view" on climate change, cap and trade, or immigration is to trivialize both the Bible and the issues. The truth is that with many of these secondary issues, the Bible can be used to support either side of an argument. For example, some proponents of universal health care point to the fact that Jesus healed people from diseases as a reason for mandating that insurance companies not exclude preexisting conditions from coverage. Using that reasoning, opponents of universal health care could argue that the Bible is against insurance since Jesus is capable of healing all diseases!

However, there are some issues to which the Bible speaks clearly. Most political pundits agree that when it comes to "values" issues such as abortion and same-sex marriage, voter fatigue has rendered these issues much less important than they were a decade ago. Nevertheless, as we saw in the first chapter, these issues are of paramount importance to the spiritual health and future survival of our nation.

Furthermore, a candidate's position on these issues reflects his view of Scripture. I accept at face value President Obama's declaration that he is a Christian. In an interview with *Christianity Today*, the president said, "I am a Christian, and I am a devout Christian. I believe in the redemptive death and resurrection of Jesus Christ. I believe that that faith gives me a path to be cleansed of sin and have eternal life."[11]

However, apparently President Obama does not find the Bible particularly helpful in giving direction for public policy. In his "Call to Renewal" speech in 2006, then Senator Obama declared:

And even if we did have only Christians in our midst, if we expelled every non-Christian from the United States of America, whose Christianity would we teach in our schools? Would we go with James Dobson's, or Al Sharpton's? Which passages of Scripture should guide our public policy? Should we go with Leviticus, which suggests slavery is ok and that eating shellfish is an abomination? How about Deuteronomy, which suggests stoning your child if he strays from the faith? Or should we just stick to the Sermon on the Mount—a passage that is so radical that it's doubtful that our own Defense Department would survive its application? So before we get carried away, let's read our [B]ibles. Folks haven't been reading their [B]ibles.[12]

President Obama apparently believes that although the Bible may be helpful for personal spiritual growth (he reportedly receives a devotion every day on his BlackBerry), he finds the Scriptures to be completely irrelevant to providing guidance for public policy. He implies in this speech that the Bible is filled with arcane, confusing, and contradictory statements that no one could possibly make sense of, much less apply to our country.

Although the subject of biblical hermeneutics (how to interpret the Bible) is beyond the scope of this book, President Obama—as well as others who make similar statements implying that the Bible is irrelevant for today—must be called out for one glaring error. Any serious student of the Bible understands that there is a difference between the Old Testament, which contains laws under which Israel lived, and the New Testament, which outlines the code of conduct for Christians today.

To reach back to Old Testament laws to prove the inadequacy of the Bible to give direction for our nation today is akin to arguing that the United States Constitution is irrelevant and ineffective because of the Eighteenth Amendment, which prohibits the consumption of alcohol. The problem with such an argument is that the Eighteenth Amendment was nullified by the Twenty-First Amendment, which repealed the prohibition against alcohol. If you want to know what the Constitution allows and prohibits regarding alcohol consumption, you read the new amendment rather than the older amendment. Likewise, to know what God allows and prohibits today one needs to read the New Testament rather than the Old Testament.

I don't know whether the president's blatant and misleading statements about the interpretation of Scripture are intentional. His comments may be the result of biblical illiteracy, or they may represent a calculated attempt to demonstrate the supposed irrelevance of the Bible for today's world. Regardless of his motives, his statements do reveal his conviction that the Bible cannot be used as a reliable guide for public policy.

President Obama is not alone in that persuasion. Anytime a politician attempts to disparage the Bible with similar statements he is telegraphing to the electorate that God's Word is incapable of providing guidance for today's issues.

## ★ Question #4: How Does He View the Constitution? ★

One of the most enduring legacies of any politician is the judges he nominates or votes to confirm. The judicial branch of our government wields enormous power because of its ability to interpret or reinterpret the law. Of course, judges are to use the United States Constitution as their guide for rendering decisions. But there are two very different schools of thought among judges and the politicians who place them on the bench regarding the nature of the Constitution and how it should be applied in today's world.

Constructionists believe that judges have the responsibility to abide by the original intent of the framers of the Constitution. Although a rapidly changing world brings new challenges in applying the Constitution to today's society, judges are charged with gauging their decisions by the timeless principles found in the Constitution. The only way those principles can be altered is through the intentionally laborious process the Founding Fathers devised for amending the Constitution.

However, a growing number of politicians and jurists have adopted an expansionist view of the Constitution. In his autobiography, *The Audacity of Hope*, President Obama accurately summarizes this view of the Constitution:

> Ultimately, though, I have to side with Justice Breyer's view of the Constitution—that it is not a static but rather a living document, and must be read in the context of an ever-changing world. How could it be otherwise? The constitutional text provides us with the general principle that we aren't subject to unreasonable searches by the government. It can't tell us the founder's spiritual views on the reasonableness of an NSA computer data-mining operation. The constitutional text tells us that freedom of speech must be protected, but it doesn't tell us what such a freedom means in the context of the Internet.[13]

While any reasonable person would conclude that judges are necessary to apply Constitutional principles to a changing culture, the question is whether those judges must abide by such principles, or are they free to invent new principles? Those who believe the Constitution is organic see it as an ever-changing body of truth. One observer said, "It's as if the Founders wrote it on a blackboard and gave judges an eraser and chalk." The result of the expansionist view of the Constitution is that the judiciary grants imaginary rights to some individuals, while depriving others of very real rights. The Supreme Court did both in *Lawrence and Garner v. Texas*, cited in chapter 2.

By striking down Texas's law against sodomy, the High Court added to the United States Constitution the right to engage in homosexual conduct, even though, as Kelly Shackelford, chief counsel for Liberty Legal Institute, notes, "There is no constitutional right to engage in homosexual sodomy. Read the Constitution as many times as you'd like. It's not there."[14] This imaginary right evolved from another bogus right that is accepted as fundamental to most Americans: the so-called right to privacy. In the landmark abortion decision *Roe v. Wade* (1973), the Supreme Court discovered somewhere hidden between the lines of the Fourteenth Amendment the "freedom from government domination in making the most intimate and personal decisions."[15] In *Roe*, the intimate and personal decision deserving Constitutional protection was murdering an unborn child. In *Lawrence*, it was sodomy. In future years it may be the intimate and personal decision to engage in sex with one's consenting child. Fortunately, a minority of Supreme Court justices such as Clarence Thomas and Anton Scalia have not yet found such a right to privacy in the Constitution.

Nevertheless, a growing number of judges are finding such imaginary rights as privacy, which usually results in the erasing of existing rights for others. For example, by reading into the Fourteenth Amendment the imaginary right of privacy, the Supreme Court usurped the clear right of individual communities and states to formulate laws through their elected officials. If a majority of citizens in Texas had disagreed with the state's anti-sodomy statute, then that law could have been changed through the legislative process. But it never was. The Supreme Court acted as a superlegislature, overriding the will of the people. In doing so, the Court discarded the very real right of a state (and its citizens) to formulate its own laws.

Many citizens assume that the federal government—and its attendant "muscle" known as the Supreme Court—have the final say on every legal issue. We have accepted the idea that the only power that individual states (and the citizens who populate those states) have is relegated to issues of secondary importance like highway beautification programs or insurance regulations.

But the framers of the Constitution never envisioned such sweeping authority for the federal government. The Tenth Amendment to the Constitution reads:

> The powers not delegated to the United States by the Constitution, nor prohibited by it to the States, are reserved to the States respectively, or to the people.

In other words, the only powers the federal government possesses are those specifically stated in the Constitution. Every other power belongs to the states and to the people, including the power to formulate laws for local communities.

An expansionist view of the Constitution can also curtail other important rights of citizens. Using the First Amendment as a pretext, some judges have invented the "right" of unbelievers to be spared from uttering the words "under God" in the pledge of allegiance, seeing a nativity scene in the town square, or hearing a prayer at a high school football game. The invention of the "right" to freedom *from* religion has resulted in the abrogation of a very real right we all have under the First Amendment to the freedom of religious expression.

Before choosing a political leader who controls or influences the selection of judges, it is important to know whether that leader is a constructionist or an expansionist regarding the Constitution. The creation of imaginary rights for the few always results in the forfeiture of real rights for the many.

## ★ You *Can* Make a Difference ★

It seems that we are in a perpetual election cycle in our country. No sooner have the ballots been counted in one election than pundits begin their endless speculation and candidates begin their accumulation of cash for the next contest. So regardless of when you pick up this book there will be another election just around the corner. As you approach an upcoming election, allow me to offer three practical exhortations.

## ★ Participate in the Process ★

In the 2008 presidential election approximately 40 percent of the 208 million eligible voters stayed home. George Gallup estimates that about 40 percent of the electorate is evangelical Christians. Given that there is no evidence that the evangelical turnout is greater than the rest of the population, that means that more than thirty million Christians did not vote in the last election. Barack Obama's victory was considered a landslide by many because he won by about ten million votes.[16] My point is not that "had more Christians voted they could have kept Obama out of the White House" (that's too partisan even for me!). But what the data does say is that Christians have the ability to heavily influence an election, which in turn determines the direction of our nation.

I am often challenged by Christians to demonstrate where in the Bible God says Christians should get involved in politics. Such a challenge fails to take into account the difference in the New Testament culture and our culture. First-century believers lived under the oppression of the Roman government. Yet Jesus instructed His followers to fulfill their obligation to the governing authorities. "Render to Caesar the things that are Caesar's," the Lord commanded (Mark 12:17). Similarly, Paul instructed the Roman Christians living under the tyrannical reign of the Roman emperor Nero to "be in subjection to the governing authorities" (Romans 13:1). In the first century Christians were living as a minority and there was no command to organize and overthrow the Roman government.

But Christians living in the United States of America two thousand years later are in a vastly different situation than the early believers. Instead of having political leaders imposed upon us, we have the unique privilege of selecting our leaders. As John Jay, the first chief justice of the Supreme Court, noted, "The Americans are the first people whom Heaven has favored with an opportunity of deliberating upon and choosing the forms of government under which they should live."[17]

With the God-given ability to select our leaders comes an inherent responsibility to participate in the process. Admittedly, a democratic republic is difficult to maintain. It is said that as Benjamin Franklin emerged from a meeting of the Constitutional Convention, a woman asked him, "Mr. Franklin, what sort of government have you given us?" Franklin answered, "A republic, madam, if you can keep it." Franklin understood that the greatest enemy of democracy is apathy. Without the involvement of citizens in the electoral process, democracy can quickly be replaced by tyranny.

Jesus' command for Christians to be the salt of the earth (Matthew 5:13) has not been repealed. We are to help preserve our world from premature decay by standing against evil. God has given Christians in democratic countries a unique way to "salt" their world that first-century believers did not enjoy. We have been granted the freedom to choose leaders that will advance righteousness or unrighteousness.

The alternative to Christians being involved in the selection of political leaders is both demonstrable and frightening. Dr. Jeff Myers notes that during the twentieth century, atheistic and secular humanistic leaders gained control of nations all across Europe, Asia, and Africa. The result? "According to historian R. J. Rummel, 'Almost 170 million men, women, and children have been shot, beaten, tortured, knifed, burned, starved, frozen, crushed, or worked to death; buried alive, drowned, hung, bombed, or killed in any other of the myriad of ways governments have inflicted death on unarmed, helpless citizens and foreigners.'"[18] Evil triumphs when Christians do nothing.

## ★ Vote on the Basis of Facts, Not Rumors ★

During the 2004 presidential election, a number of people forwarded an e-mail to me about an incident that supposedly took place at a campaign rally. Democratic nominee John Kerry, supposedly trying to pander to Christians, talked about his favorite verse in the Bible. But instead of citing John 3:16, Kerry said his favorite verse was John 16:3. According to the e-mail, Kerry and his advisers were so unfamiliar with the Bible that they did not know the difference. The punch line of the story is that in John 16:3 Jesus says, "These things they will do because they have not known the Father or Me." Chuckle, chuckle.

The only problem with that story is that it didn't happen—not to John Kerry. The very same story made the rounds during the 2000 election about Democratic nominee Al Gore. It didn't happen to him either. But the story does have some basis in fact. A presidential candidate did accidentally cite John 16:3 rather than John 3:16 as his favorite verse. His name? George H. W. Bush. In 1988 while running for president, then Vice President Bush made the gaffe while addressing the National Religious Broadcasters convention.

Before we accept a story as true—and send it to everyone on our e-mail list—we should ask ourselves, "Do I know for sure that this information is correct?" As Christians we have the responsibility of "laying aside falsehood" and to "speak truth" as Paul commanded in Ephesians 4:25. One good way to discover the validity of a story that seems to be a little too fantastic to be true is by utilizing the website UrbanLegends.com.

More importantly, if you want to know how candidates stand on the issues, don't allow the media—conservative or liberal—to tell you what a candidate believes. Instead, use a reputable voters' guide such as the ones published by Liberty Legal Institute or Family Research Council. These guides are prepared through questionnaires completed by the candidates themselves (or in some cases, public statements made by the candidates) and reveal their positions on a variety of issues.

Elections are too important to be decided by rumor or innuendo. We need to base our decisions on fact, not fiction.

## ★ Trust in God's Sovereignty ★

As representatives of the King of kings, Christians need to stop hyperventilating during every election and making hysterical comments such as, "If so-and-so is elected, it will be the end of our country!" Remember, God is not seated on His throne biting his nails over any election. God already knows the outcome, because He has determined the outcome. God is the one who "removes kings and establishes kings" (Daniel 2:21). He is the one who establishes every government of every nation that has ever existed (Romans 13:1).

Now, don't use God's control over elections as an excuse for passivity. Yes, God has ordained the outcome for every election. But God has also ordained the means to achieve that outcome—your and my exercise of our responsibility to vote. Nevertheless, as Christians who are trying to serve as a positive witness for Christ, we should avoid any hint of panic, fear, or lack of faith in God when we talk about an upcoming election.

Why should Christians involve themselves in the political process? Elected officials determine the direction of our nation by the laws they enact. Those who say Christians should not try to impose their morality on the populace or that we should not try to legislate morality forget one important fact that Charles Colson highlighted in a radio commentary:

> As citizens of the kingdom of God, Christians are to bring God's standards of righteousness and justice to bear on the kingdoms of this world—what is sometimes called the cultural commission. Among other things, this means bringing transcendent moral values into public debate.
>
> The popular notion that "you can't legislate morality" is a myth. Morality is legislated every day from the vantage point of one value system being chosen over another. The question is not whether we will legislate morality, but *whose* morality gets legislated.[19] (emphasis added)

Those who argue that Christians do not need to become individually or corporately involved in politics need to ask themselves:

- Does God care whether unborn children are allowed to be murdered?
- Does God care whether sexual immorality is sanctioned by the state?
- Does God care whether any mention of His name is outlawed in the public square?
- Does God care whether righteous or unrighteous people govern our nation?

The answers to those questions reveal both why and how a Christian should vote. Those answers also provide the foundation for understanding both why and how pastors need to mobilize their churches to be agents of righteousness—the focus of the next chapter.

# CHAPTER
# 5

## For Pastors Only

You may recall that special day in the fifth or sixth grade when boys and girls were separated and taken to individual rooms to receive some special information about their changing bodies. While most of us were relatively attentive to the sometimes confusing facts we were hearing, we (especially us boys) were extremely curious about what was going on in the other room with the members of the opposite sex! There is something downright titillating about information that is restricted.

I admit that by titling this chapter "For Pastors Only," I am seeking to capitalize on that innate curiosity we have for information reserved for a specific group of people. However, the content of this chapter—while directly addressed to those who lead local churches—is applicable to every Christian who is concerned about the future of our nation. The thesis of this chapter is quite simple: The preservation of our nation for the proclamation of the gospel depends upon the effectiveness of local congregations in fulfilling their mission. And the effectiveness of local congregations in fulfilling their mission depends upon pastors fulfilling their calling.

## ★ No Respect ★

The late comedian Rodney Dangerfield and the local church share one common trait: both "get no respect," as Dangerfield used to lament about himself. Recently, a congregation in our community that targets young adults erected a billboard on the freeway that read "Come and see, not our church, but our Christ." The not-so-subtle message is that there is something about the organization of the local church that distracts people from seeing Jesus Christ, even though the New Testament repeatedly refers to the church as "the body of Christ." Disdain for the local church is everywhere. The other night while waiting for a movie to begin, I saw a commercial for another local church that began with these words: "What do you think of when you hear the word 'church'? Judgmental? Irrelevant? You're probably right . . ."

What is deeply disturbing to me is that the newest wave of assault against the local church is not coming from unbelievers, but from Christian leaders. One pastor wrote:

> Sitting down with a friend over coffee is every bit as spiritual as going to church together. The casual setting provides just as great an opportunity for supernatural influence as being in church does—and often even more.[1]

If there is no more value to attending church than sitting down with a friend for coffee, why in the world should I go through the hassle of getting up early on Sunday morning and hauling my family to a worship service? Why give sacrificially to an organization like the church if my local Starbucks is doing just as much to advance the kingdom of God?

Some Christian leaders are not only questioning the value of the local church, but they are actually identifying the church as a hindrance to spiritual growth. A best-selling Christian author wrote about a dry period in his spiritual life that he attributed in some part to his involvement in church. What advice does he offer others who might be traveling through their own spiritual Sahara?

> You might even need to give up going to church for a while or reading your Bible. I stopped going to church for a year; it was one of the most refreshing years of my life. I hadn't abandoned God, and I very much sought out the company of my spiritual companions. What I gave up was the performance of having to show up every Sunday morning with my happy face on.[2]

With leaders like these disparaging the need for the church, no wonder church attendance continues to decline.

Futurist George Barna predicts that the decline will continue. Within a few years "millions of people will never travel physically to a church, but will instead roam the Internet in search of meaningful spiritual experiences."[3] That seems to be all right with Barna since the essence of Christianity is the development of people's character.[4] Spiritual transformation or even intimate worship does "not require a 'worship service'" but a personal commitment to the spiritual disciplines.[5]

I will be the first to admit that the local church is filled with flaws. I can identify with Mark Buchanan, who writes:

> I assume you're like me: I can get itchy-skinned and scratchy-throated after an hour or so of church. I can get distracted and cranky when it goes too long. My feet ache, my backside numbs, my eyes glaze, my mind fogs, my belly growls. I find myself fighting back yawns, and then not fighting them back, letting them gape and roar, a signal to my oppressors: **Let my people go.** And I'm the pastor.[6]

Yet those who write off the local church as an antiquated organization that needs to be replaced by a new paradigm for spiritual transformation forget one important fact: the local church was created by God, not man, to achieve His purpose in the world. The idea of the church, the mission of the church, the composition of the church, the organization of the church, and the priority of the church are all outlined in Scripture. Why do Christians—and especially those in high-profile leadership positions within the evangelical community—feel empowered to alter or delete the biblical mandates about that organization that was birthed out of the death of Jesus Christ?

## ★ God's Plan for the Church ★

The centrality of the church in fulfilling God's purpose in the world is seen throughout Scripture. A year ago when our congregation unveiled its plan for our new campus in downtown Dallas, fellow pastor and friend Jack Graham sent me a text message before the service:

> Now to Him who is able to do far more abundantly beyond all that we ask or think, according to the power that works within us, to Him be the glory in the church and in Christ Jesus to all generations forever and ever. Amen. (Ephesians 3:20–21)

How is God exalted in the world today? In the church and in Christ Jesus. The church is the visible representation of Jesus Christ in the world.

The congregation that implied through its billboard that the church was somehow an impediment to seeing Christ forgot that Jesus is no longer in the world to be seen as He was during his thirty-three years of life on earth. He has left the building, so to speak, and is now sitting at the right hand of God the Father.

Until He returns to reclaim this world for Himself, Christ created the church to be His stand-in. People might try to imagine Christ in their own minds, but the only way to actually "see" Christ is by seeing His body, the church. No wonder that Christ has such an abiding affection for and interest in the church. "Christ . . . loved the church and gave Himself up for her," Paul reminded the Ephesians (5:25).

Think about this. If you were getting ready to leave on a long trip to a foreign country and were going to empower an individual to oversee all of your financial transactions, take over your job or business, and care for your family, wouldn't you have more than a passing interest in the character and the competency of that individual?

Jesus Christ has turned over something even more valuable than money, career, or family to His followers. Dorothy Sayers has written that God has undergone three great acts of humiliation in human history. The first was the incarnation, when He poured Himself into the confines of a human body. The second was the crucifixion, when He suffered the humiliation of a public execution by His own subjects. The third humiliation, Sayers declares, is the church, through which God has entrusted his reputation to ordinary people.[7]

Whenever I write or speak about the centrality of the church in God's plan, someone usually offers this objection: "Don't you realize that when the New Testament speaks of the church it is referring to all Christians everywhere, not to a local congregation?" Yes, I understand the concept of what theologians term the universal church, which is comprised of all believers who have trusted in Christ since the Day of Pentecost. Many who are part of that universal congregation are already in the presence of Christ, while the rest of us reside temporarily on earth.

But of the more than one hundred references to the word "church" in the New Testament, ninety of those references are to local congregations, not the universal church. It is through individual congregations planted in local communities throughout the world that God's purposes ultimately will be realized.

Certainly one of those purposes is the spiritual transformation of individual believers into the image of Christ that Barna and others have highlighted. However, such transformation is best achieved in a community of believers rather than in isolation. To become like Christ we need sound teaching from Scripture, so God has given to every local congregation those who are equipped to be:

. . . pastors and teachers, for the equipping of the saints for the work of service, to the building up of the body of Christ. (Ephesians 4:11-12)

Beyond instruction from the Bible, believers need to learn how to forgive those who wrong us, place other people's interests above our own, and take care of those who are in need if we are going to be imitators of Christ. Trust me, you will learn *none* of those things on the Internet! What better place to develop forgiveness, humility, and sacrifice than in a local congregation?

After more than thirty years of service in the local church, I have changed my mind about conflicts in the church. I used to view disagreements in churches as harmful distractions, but now I see them as potential catalysts for spiritual transformation. You can't learn to forgive someone unless you are first hurt by someone. You can't learn how to surrender your preferences if you are always in agreement with everyone. The local church serves as an incubator to foster spiritual growth.

## ★ Beyond Transformation ★

God's purposes do not stop with our own spiritual development. He is just as concerned about the well-being of other believers as He is about yours, and that is why He designed the local church. God understands that because believers are a minority in the world, they need the encouragement that comes from other Christians if they are to remain steadfast in their own faith. The author of Hebrews addressed believers who were living in a darkening culture that was hostile to the faith:

Let us hold fast the confession of our hope without wavering, for He who promised is faithful; and let us consider how to stimulate one another to love and good deeds, not forsaking our own assembling together, as is the habit of some, but encouraging one another; and all the more as you see the day drawing near. (Hebrews 10:23–25)

Assembling together in individual communities of faith called the church is not optional but essential if we are to persevere in our relationship with God. Nelson Mandela illustrates the inherent power of a group bound together by the same beliefs, especially when that group is facing persecution. Mandela and a group of political prisoners spent almost thirty years in captivity on Robben Island. In his autobiography *Long Walk to Freedom,* Mandela describes the relationships that were strengthened during their imprisonment:

The authorities' greatest mistake was to keep us together, for together our determination was reinforced. We supported each other and gained strength from each other. Whatever we knew, whatever we learned, we shared, and by sharing we multiplied whatever courage we had individually. That is not to say that we were all alike in our responses to the hardships we suffered. Men have different capacities and react differently to stress. But the stronger ones raised up the weaker ones, and both became stronger in the process.[8]

Mandela's experience illustrates Solomon's observation:

Two are better than one because they have a good return for their labor. For if either of them falls, the one will lift up his companion. But woe to the one who falls when there is not another to lift him up. (Ecclesiastes 4:9–10)

Those who diminish the importance of the local church and only emphasize individual spiritual transformation forget that interaction with other believers in the setting God has designed is crucial for our own spiritual fidelity, especially during those inevitable times of testing. There is strength in numbers!

## ★ It's Not About Us ★

God's purposes for the world ultimately extend beyond our and other believers' individual spiritual growth. Just as God formed the nation of Israel to be His representatives on earth under the old covenant, God has created the church to proclaim His truth and reflect His holiness in the world today. As Peter reminded the first-century believers:

But you are A CHOSEN RACE, a royal PRIESTHOOD, A HOLY NATION, A PEOPLE FOR GOD'S OWN POSSESSION, so that you may proclaim the excellencies of Him who has called you out of darkness into His marvelous light. (1 Peter 2:9)

Instead of creating one massive organization called The Church with one designated leader, God's plan was to blanket the globe with individual communities of believers who would serve as His representatives. Many of the books of the New Testament are actually letters addressed to local congregations in cities such as Corinth, Ephesus, and Colossae. Each church had its own set of problems as well as unique opportunities.

Recently I finished preaching a year-long series on the book of the Revelation, a letter addressed to seven local congregations identified in the opening chapters. Eugene Peterson writes that when he served as a pastor he was often frustrated by the imperfections and immaturity of his congregation, especially when compared to the ideal pattern for the church described in the New Testament. But then Peterson noticed something in the book of the Revelation.

The seven churches identified as the recipients of this letter were far from the ideal! In fact, six of them received firm reprimands from God—some for immorality, others for apathy, and even one for apostasy! Nevertheless, these churches were described as "lampstands" by God in the dark world in which first-century Christians resided. "They are places, locations where the light of Christ is shown," writes Peterson. "They are not themselves the light. There is nothing particularly glamorous about churches, nor, on the other hand, is there anything particularly shameful about them. They simply are."[9]

God has placed local churches in every community as part of a larger lampstand illuminating His glory and His truth in a dark world. Unfortunately, we often interpret Jesus' reminder that "you are the light of the world" through our Western mind-set of individualism. We picture ourselves as carrying around our own candles as we sing, "This little light of mine, I'm going to let it shine," trying to be a positive witness for Christ wherever we are. But as helpful as an individual light can be at times, there is something even more impressive and powerful when lots of little lights come together to form a floodlight.

I used to illustrate that truth every year at our church's annual candlelight Christmas Eve service (until the fire marshal required us to use electric candles). At the end of Communion the congregation would sing "Silent Night" in a completely darkened sanctuary. I would light my candle and then light the candles of our ushers, who in turn would light the candles of those on the end of each pew. Within a few minutes several thousand candles being held up together totally dispelled the darkness of the sanctuary. Once we finished singing, I would invite the congregation to look at the brilliance of thousands of individual lights shining together as one.

God designed the local church to be a community of individual lights that are organized to form a larger light to illuminate the holiness and truth of God. A community of Christians can more effectively salt their world with righteousness than if they only act as individual grains. A body of believers can more effectively illuminate the gospel message in their community than they can as individual penlights. When it comes to illumination, two lights really are better than one!

But the effectiveness of the local church in fulfilling its unique mission depends upon pastors fulfilling their unique calling. Why? John Maxwell refers to "The Law of the Lid" in his book *The Twenty-One Irrefutable Laws of Leadership*. Simply stated, no organization ever rises above its leader. The leader is the lid of any organization.[10] I realize that it is fashionable today to diminish the importance of the pastor in the local congregation, assuming that his calling is no different than that of anyone else in the congregation. However, the Bible refers to the pastor as the "overseer" of the church (1 Timothy 3:1).

When God had a message to deliver to each of the seven churches mentioned in Revelation 2–3, He did not address the letters to the pastoral oversight committee at the church of Sardis or even to the elders at the church of Sardis. Instead, the letters were addressed to individual pastors or "angels" (meaning, "messengers") at each church. Regardless of the debate over church polity that has raged since the birth of the church, the fact remains that every organization must have a leader. As the late Adrian Rogers used to say, "Anything with no head is dead and anything with two heads is a freak!"[11] While Jesus Christ is the invisible Head of the universal church, He has appointed individual pastors of individual congregations to serve as "heads" or leaders of local congregations.

Pastor, remember that leadership of the church is not a privilege to be exploited but a sobering responsibility to be fulfilled. God holds pastors responsible for the spiritual well-being of the members of your church. Too many pastors know only the first portion of Hebrews 13:17: "Obey your leaders and submit to them." However, the reason members are to follow the leadership of their pastors causes me to lay awake at nights:

Obey your leaders, and submit to them, *for they keep watch over your souls as those who will give an account.* Let them do this with joy and not with grief, for this would be unprofitable for you. (Hebrews 13:17; emphasis added)

Every shepherd of every local congregation will one day give an account to God for the spiritual health of those placed under his care.

Beyond the spiritual health of individual members of our congregation, we pastors will also be held responsible for the overall effectiveness of our church:

Shepherd the flock of God among you, exercising oversight not under compulsion, but voluntarily, according to the will of God; and not for sordid gain, but with eagerness; nor yet as lording it over those allotted to your charge, but proving to be examples to the flock. And when the Chief Shepherd appears, you will receive the unfading crown of glory. (1 Peter 5:2–4)

This passage strongly indicates that those of us who have been given temporary charge over a local congregation will give an account one day to the Chief Shepherd concerning our stewardship of that local body of believers. Have we led our congregation to fulfill its God-given mandate to be salt and light in the communities in which we have been placed?

Eugene Peterson accurately describes the end result of pastors who do not understand their unique calling:

American pastors are abandoning their posts, left and right, and at an alarming rate. They are not leaving their churches and getting other jobs. Congregations still pay their salaries. Their names remain on the church stationery and they continue to appear in pulpits on Sundays. But they are abandoning their posts, their *calling*. They have gone whoring after other gods. What they do with their time under the guise of pastoral ministry hasn't the remotest connection with what the church's pastors have done for most of twenty centuries. . . .

The pastors of America have metamorphosed into a company of shopkeepers, and the shops they keep are churches. They are preoccupied with shopkeeper's concerns—how to keep the customers happy, how to lure customers away from competitors down the street, how to package the goods so that the customers will lay out more money.

Some of them are very good shopkeepers. They attract a lot of customers, pull in great sums of money, develop splendid reputations. Yet it is still shopkeeping: religious shop shopkeeping, to be sure, but shopkeeping all the same.[12]

If Christians are going to seize the unique opportunity that our decaying and darkening cultural landscape provides, it will be through hundreds of thousands of vibrant local communities of believers that dot the globe. But these individual communities of believers—called the church—will only be as effective as the pastors who lead them. To effectively lead a church, a pastor must abandon the "shopkeeper" mentality Peterson describes and embrace the three roles every pastor is called to fulfill.

## ★ The Pastor as Preacher ★

I realize that the word *preach* is used primarily in a pejorative way today. "Don't preach at people; talk to them," seminary students are instructed. "Papa, don't preach," Madonna pleaded in a popular song years ago. "You're preaching again," my daughters used to lament whenever I would offer a piece of advice. If not treated with outright contempt, the task of preaching is increasingly diminished. Someone was describing her pastor to me recently: "He's not a very good preacher, but he's a great pastor." That's like describing a surgeon by saying, "He's not very good with a knife, but he has a great bedside manner." That's not a doctor you would likely choose for a major operation!

The pastor's primary duty is not vision-casting, managing, strategizing, or comforting, but preaching. Read carefully Paul's sobering command to his spiritual protégé, Timothy, who served as pastor of the church at Ephesus:

> I solemnly charge you in the presence of God and of Christ Jesus, who is to judge the living and the dead, and by His appearing and His kingdom: preach the word; be ready in season and out of season; reprove, rebuke, exhort, with great patience and instruction. (2 Timothy 4:1–2)

The word "preach" used in this passage means "to herald, to proclaim." In Paul's day, the herald was the emperor's representative charged with delivering the emperor's message. The clarifying words "reprove, rebuke, exhort" carry a sense of urgency with which we are to deliver God's message. To "reprove" means to speak persuasively. To "rebuke" means to speak out against wrongdoing. And to "exhort" means to come alongside people and encourage them.

Preaching involves more than conversing or dialoguing with people about spiritual issues. The pastor is to passionately proclaim his message to fulfill his calling. A discouraged pastor once asked the prince of preachers, Charles Spurgeon, what to do to draw the same kind of crowd Spurgeon was attracting. "Simply douse yourself in gasoline, strike a match, and set yourself on fire," replied Spurgeon. "Then people will come to watch you burn." [13] Preaching is the art of setting truth on fire.

Paul's command was not simply to "preach" but to "preach the Word." The emperor's herald did not have the liberty to compose his own message. Instead, his job was to proclaim the message that had been entrusted to him by the emperor. Unfortunately, many pastors have forgotten that simple truth. Every Sunday morning while downing several cups of coffee to jump-start my heart, I flip through the television channels looking at various pastors. The other day I watched a pastor who is a very effective communicator. He was standing on a stage in front of an elaborately designed set constructed to coincide with his message about living life to the fullest. The message was well crafted and masterfully delivered. The crowd of many thousands listened attentively. Yet the pastor never once referenced a verse from Scripture. As I listened I thought of Walt Kaiser's penetrating criticism of that kind of "preaching":

> Too often the Bible is little more than a book of epigrammatic sayings or springboards that give us a rallying point around which to base our editorials. But where did we get the audacious idea that God would bless our opinions or judgments? Who wants to hear another point of view as an excuse for a Bible study or a message from the Word of God? Who said God would bless our studies, our programs for the church, or our ramblings on the general area announced by the text? Surely this is a major reason why the famine of the Word continues in massive proportions in most places in North America. Surely this is why the hunger for the teaching and proclamation of God's Word continues to grow year after year. Men and women cannot live by ideas alone, no matter how eloquently they are stated or argued, but solely by a patient reading and explanation of all Scripture, line after line, paragraph after paragraph, chapter after chapter, and book after book. Where are such interpreters to be found, and where are their teachers?[14]

### ★ What Does It Mean to "Preach the Word"? ★

Paul reminded the Philippian Christians that they were to "appear as lights in the world, holding fast the word of life" (Philippians 2:15–16). It is God's Word, not our musings, that illuminates the world and points people to Christ. The church's ability to "hold fast the word of life" depends on the pastor's ability and willingness to equip his congregation with the timeless truths from God's Word. The *Westminster Directory* (1645) gives this simple definition of preaching:

> The true idea of preaching is that the preacher should become a mouthpiece for his text, opening it up and applying it as a word from God to his hearers , . . . in order that the text may speak . . . and be heard, making each point from his text in such a manner "that [his audience] may discern [the voice of God]."[15]

Sadly, a number of pastors have concluded that this kind of preaching is no longer effective. Feeling the pressure to add to or simply retain their congregation, many pastors have abandoned their unique calling and preach messages each Sunday that could just as easily be delivered by Deepak Chopra. Entertainment rather than exposition has become the end goal of many pastors. As John Piper observes:

> Laughter seems to have replaced repentance as the goal of many preachers. Laughter means people feel good. It means they like you, it means you have . . . some measure of power. It seems to have all the marks of successful communication—if the depth of sin and the holiness of God and the danger of hell and the need for broken hearts is left out of account.[16]

The temptation to entertain rather than equip church members is nothing new. Paul's admonition to Timothy to "preach the Word" was coupled with this sobering reminder:

For the time will come when they will not endure sound doctrine; but wanting to have their ears tickled, they will accumulate for themselves teachers in accordance to their own desires, and will turn away their ears from the truth and will turn aside to myths. But you, be sober in all things, endure hardship . . . fulfill your ministry. (2 Timothy 4:3–5)

One of the seminaries I attended had as its motto Paul's exhortation "Preach the Word." I will be eternally indebted to the wonderful training I received from godly and gifted professors in that institution. However, there was an implicit message from many professors that if we as pastors will simply preach the Word, our churches will automatically grow to such numbers that we will not be able to contain the crowds. Chapel speakers—usually famous alumni from that institution—would underscore that message by relating how their congregations grew from a few hundred to thousands of members because of their faithful exposition of the Scriptures.

After seminary, I went to pastor my first church in a small town in West Texas and began preaching through the Bible, book by book, just as I had been instructed. I wondered how soon it would be before I needed to appoint a building committee to construct a larger auditorium to accommodate what soon would be capacity crowds. It never happened.

During the seven years I was there I did preach God's Word faithfully. The attendance declined at times, other times it grew, and sometimes it simply plateaued. It took many years for me to realize that when I stood before Jesus Christ to give an account of my stewardship as a pastor, the Lord was not going to pull out a graph and review the numerical growth of my congregation. Those of us who are pastors will be evaluated on the basis of our faithfulness in proclaiming God's Word, not on our success in building a large church.

Pastor, if you truly want the congregation with which God has entrusted you to be a light that points people to Jesus Christ, I join with the apostle Paul in pleading with you to stop trying to be popular with everyone, quit obsessing over how many people are attending your services, and give up trying to imitate the growth strategies of other congregations. Instead, preach the Word. What makes the proclamation of God's Word so powerful?

## ★ God's Word Has the Power to Save ★

Someone once asked G. K. Chesterton, "If you were marooned on a desert island and could have only one book, which would you choose?" The questioner, knowing Chesterton's Christian beliefs, probably expected him to answer, "The Bible." Instead, Chesterton answered, "Thomas' Guide to Practical Ship Building."[17] Great answer! After all, if you are stranded on an island, your priority is getting off the island.

All mankind is spiritually shipwrecked. We are trapped on this sin-infected planet and desperately need a way to return to the God who created us and loves us. Only the Bible provides the direction we need to find our way home. As our culture becomes increasingly pluralistic and views all religions as equally viable spiritual choices, it is imperative that we pastors boldly and passionately proclaim that salvation comes only through faith in Jesus Christ.

Now let me say something to pastors that may offend others who are reading this book. You must make the proclamation of God's Word the priority in your worship service. I have a pastor friend who lamented to me, "Our worship leader takes the first forty-five minutes of the service and leaves me with just fifteen minutes to preach." I told that pastor that it was time to have a frank discussion with the worship leader about the centrality of God's Word in the service.

I am a strong believer in the importance of good music in a worship service. However, while people may be drawn to the gospel by a song, a personal testimony, or a moving video, the Holy Spirit uses the Word of God to produce life in a heart that is spiritually dead. As James wrote, it is the "word implanted, which is able to save your souls" (James 1:21). Make sure that the focal point of every worship service is the proclamation of God's Word.

## ★ The Power to Heal ★

What is the root cause of the failed marriages, enslaving addictions, unresolved bitterness, and unending anxiety that are so characteristic of our culture? "Sin," you would probably answer—and you would be right. But the natural follow-up question is, "What is the root cause of sin that results in the destruction of our lives?" Wrong thinking always leads to wrong behavior. As the Bible says, "For as [a person] thinks within himself, so he is" (Proverbs 23:7).

- We think we are responsible for our future, so we are bound up with anxiety.
- We think money is the key to happiness, so we are bound up in greed.
- We think faithfulness to our mate will lead to boredom, so we are bound up in immoral thoughts, habits, and actions.

- We think revenge is the best response to mistreatment from others, so we are bound up in bitterness.

People can spend years trying to free themselves from these wrong patterns of thinking through therapy, support groups, books, or New Year's resolutions. However, God offers a much more effective tool to free us from the wrong thoughts and behaviors that enslave us:

For the word of God is living and active and sharper than any two-edged sword, and piercing as far as the division of soul and spirit, of both joints and marrow, and able to judge the thoughts and intentions of the heart. (Hebrews 4:12)

Every time I read that passage I am reminded of the legend of Gordius, who tied a knot with such complexity that no one was able to unravel it. Then Alexander the Great came along and simply pulled out his sword and sliced the knot in two! God's Word has a way of slicing through the complex and seemingly unanswerable dilemmas that entangle our lives. The Word of God is sharper than any "two-edged sword." The Roman two-edged sword was a powerful instrument of destruction. A Roman soldier would slice his victim in one direction and then flail the sword in the opposite direction to finish the job.

Yet God's Word is even more powerful than the Roman sword because it has the power to unravel the wrong "thoughts and intentions of the heart" that enslave us to sin. It is through God's Word that "all things are open and laid bare to the eyes of Him with whom we have to do" (Hebrews 4:13).

However, unlike the Roman soldier who sliced and diced his victims to destroy them, God is more like a surgeon who opens up His patients to heal them. As God reminded the Israelites:

See now that I, I am He, and there is no god besides Me; it is I who put to death and give life. I have wounded and it is I who heal, and there is no one who can deliver from My hand. (Deuteronomy 32:39)

This past Sunday a member of our church approached me after the service and said, "I have been anxious all week about the possibility of cancer. My husband said, 'Call Robert and talk with him,' but I didn't want to bother you. Instead I asked God to use something in your message today to give me some relief from this constant fear that I was going to die. You quoted Psalm 139:16 about all of our days being written in God's book and you said that we do not leave this earth one minute earlier or later than God has planned. That is just the word I needed today! Now, tell me the truth. My husband called you, didn't he?" I laughed and assured her he hadn't. He didn't need to. God uses His Word to bring conviction and healing to the human heart.

## ★ The Power to Transform ★

While God is vitally interested in the collective power of local churches, He is also interested in the individuals who make up the body of Christ. God's overriding purpose for every believer is clearly stated in Romans 8:29:

For those whom He foreknew, He also predestined to become conformed to the image of His Son, so that He would be the first-born among many brethren.

Listen carefully to the messages from many pulpits across our country, and you will assume that God's primary desire for your life is that you build a successful career, experience a fulfilling marriage, or enjoy a long and healthy life. None of those objectives is God's primary purpose for your life. God's one desire for you is that you mirror the attitudes, actions, and affections of His Son, Jesus Christ. In fact, in the preceding verse, Paul teaches that everything that happens in your life is orchestrated by God to achieve that result:

> And we know that God causes all things to work together for good to those who love God, to those who are called according to His purpose. (Romans 8:28)

The good for which all things in your life are working together is God's ultimate purpose for your life. God is using every success, as well as every failure, every joy, and every disappointment to make you more like the Son with whom He is so greatly pleased.

But circumstances alone don't transform us into the image of Jesus Christ. In order to remove the grime of sin that mars the image of Christ in every believer, God needs to give us a spiritual bath, using both the "water" and "soap" Paul describes:

> . . . so that He might sanctify her, having cleansed her by the washing of water with the word, that He might present to Himself the church in all her glory, having no spot or wrinkle or any such thing; but that she would be holy and blameless. (Ephesians 5:26–27)

The phrase "washing of water" refers to the power of the Holy Spirit in a Christian's life. But taking a shower or bath with water alone won't get the job done. Soap is also necessary for cleanliness, which is why Paul adds "the washing of the water with the word." God uses both His Spirit and His Word to wash away everything in our lives that is not like His Son, Jesus Christ. Since every pastor is responsible for the spiritual hygiene of his congregation, it is essential that he understand his responsibility to "lather up" his members each week with God's Word.

Noted British scholar and biblical expositor John R. W. Stott was asked if he had changed his mind about the importance of preaching. He responded:

> To the contrary! I still believe that preaching is the key to the renewal of the church. I am an impenitent believer in the power of preaching. I know all the arguments against it—that the television age has rendered preaching useless, that we are a spectator generation, that people are bored with the spoken word, disenchanted with any communication by spoken words alone. . . . Nevertheless, when a man of God stands before the people of God with the Word of God in his hand and the Spirit of God in his heart, you have a unique opportunity for communication. . . . If it is true that a human being cannot live by bread only, but by every word which proceeds out of the mouth of God, then it is also true of churches. Churches live, grow, and thrive in response to the Word of God.[18]

## ★ The Pastor as Prophet ★

My experience has been that the world in general is fairly comfortable with pastors fulfilling their roles as preachers. Even the most ardent atheist is not opposed to pastors propagating what he considers to be myths to those in the pew who are willing to listen to such nonsense. But those outside the church—and many within the church—become agitated whenever the pastor begins to confront the culture with the truth of God's Word. It's one thing for pastors to talk about building self-esteem, experiencing strong marriages, and even understanding the end times. But when a pastor criticizes a city council for approving a topless bar in his community, calls for the board of education to adopt textbooks that present a balanced view of evolution, or organizes a protest in front of a local abortion clinic, he is accused of neglecting his primary calling for "politics."

The Old Testament prophets refused to compartmentalize their message. They not only spoke to individuals about their personal relationship with God, but they also confronted their cultures as a whole for their departure from the commands of God. George Stibitz writes:

> Thus Isaiah, Hosea, Amos, Micah, and probably also Zephaniah, living at the time when false religion was bearing its natural fruit in the lives of rulers and people, laid emphasis on the demand for social purity and truthfulness by ruthlessly letting the light of publicity shine on the festering sores of the body politic. They constantly threatened national captivity as the necessary outcome of such criminality; but not without pointing to apostasy from Jehovah as the ultimate root of all evils. . . . They did not recognize the modern divorce between religion, and especially the ministerial office, on the one hand, and social and national duties on the other.[19]

In the Old Testament, a prophet was simply a man who confronted his culture with God's Word. He realized that God's interests and rule extended beyond the walls of the tabernacle or temple to include all of His creation. What leads us to believe that God's interests have changed? While God's methods may vary throughout history, His character never changes.

## ★ Why Don't Pastors Fulfill Their Prophetic Role? ★

I believe there are at least three reasons that pastors have become reluctant to fulfill their role as prophets, boldly confronting both citizens and government leaders with, "Thus saith the Lord."

## ★ A Misunderstanding of the Bible ★

When citing Old Testament prophets as a model for the pastor's prophetic role today, some will point out the differences between Israel and the church. "Israel was a theocracy. When the prophets railed against kings for the ungodly policies and citizens for unholy behavior, they were still speaking to God's own people," the argument goes. Yet prophets like Jonah, Nahum, Daniel, and John the Baptist also confronted Gentile rulers and people with God's Word and reminded them of the dire consequences of disobeying God's commands.

Others point to 1 Corinthians 5:12–13 as a reason pastors should only raise their prophetic ire against Christians within the church:

For what have I to do with judging outsiders? Do you not judge those who are within the church? But those who are outside, God judges. REMOVE THE WICKED MAN FROM AMONG YOURSELVES.

However, the context is key to understanding what Paul is teaching here. The Corinthian church was refusing to exercise discipline against a member who was blatantly involved in sexual immorality and hurting the witness of the Corinthian church. In a previous letter, Paul had instructed the Corinthians to exercise church discipline and remove unrepentant members from the congregation. Instead, the Corinthians had decided to judge non-Christians by isolating themselves from unbelievers in the world. So Paul had to clarify his instruction:

> I wrote you in my letter not to associate with immoral people; I did not at all mean with the immoral people of this world, or with the covetous and swindlers, or with idolaters, for then you would have to go out of the world. But actually, I wrote to you not to associate with any so-called brother if he is an immoral person.... For what have I to do with judging outsiders? Do you not judge those who are within the church? (1 Corinthians 5:9–12)

To "judge" unbelievers means to execute a sentence against them (in this case, isolation). Obviously, the church has no such authority against non-Christians. The church can only exercise discipline against its own members. However, Paul's instruction in no way nullifies Christians' responsibility to speak out against policies and behavior that are contrary to God's Word.

## ★ A Misunderstanding of the Constitution ★

Some pastors and many laymen believe that the so-called separation of church and state prohibits pastors from addressing controversial issues like abortion and same-sex marriages, because such topics are political rather than spiritual. Obviously, any policy or behavior that violates God's Word is a spiritual issue. Furthermore, the phrase *separation of church and state* never appears in the Constitution. Thomas Jefferson borrowed this phrase from Roger Williams in a letter Jefferson sent to a group of Baptists, trying to allay their fears that President Jefferson was about to establish a state church in America. Neither Roger Williams nor Thomas Jefferson ever used the phrase to suggest that pastors and their churches should not be involved in influencing the spiritual direction of the nation through political advocacy.

Nevertheless, there is a concerted effort today by groups such as Americans United for the Separation of Church and State and the American Civil Liberties Union to intimidate pastors and their churches from attempting to influence legislation and elections by threatening their tax-exempt status. I have been the recipient of such threats through the years and have noticed that they are almost always (though not exclusively) directed at conservative pastors.

In one sermon I urged church members to vote for Christian candidates in a city council election and the ACLU protested, even though Supreme Court Chief Justice John Jay said it is our duty to "prefer Christians" for public office.[20] On another occasion, I urged the passage of a policy for our local library that would place pro-homosexual children's books in the adult section. Again, I was threatened with the loss of our church's tax-exempt status because I was attempting to influence legislation.

What are pastors allowed to do when it comes to influencing elections or legislation? Historically, churches in our country have spoken passionately for and against candidates for public office. From the birth of our nation, pastors preached against Thomas

Jefferson for being a deist and against William Howard Taft for embracing Unitarianism. Churches have also been at the forefront of significant social changes including ending segregation and abusive child labor practices, along with advancing civil rights. However, in 1934 the government enacted a law prohibiting tax-exempt nonprofit institutions from using a "substantial" portion of their resources to lobby for legislation. That standard still applies today and in no way restricts pastors and churches from speaking for or against specific legislation as long as they do not spend a significant amount of money in doing so.

In 1954, Congress approved an amendment introduced by then Senator Lyndon Johnson to the IRS, regulations governing churches and other 501(c)(3) organizations that prohibited such organizations from seeking to influence elections by supporting specific candidates. In 1987, the amendment was expanded to also prohibit speaking out against specific candidates. Although pastors and their churches are free to influence legislation (as long as such efforts do not consume a "substantial" portion of their income), they cannot as an organization support one candidate over another in an election. As I write these words, this restriction is being challenged and many predict it will one day be repealed.

While a handful of churches have been fined for violation of these rules, *no* church has ever permanently lost its tax-exempt status in the fifty-seven years since the Johnson Amendment was added to the IRS code. The Church at Pierce Creek in Binghamton, New York, had its tax-exempt letter ruling revoked for running full-page ads in newspapers denouncing Bill Clinton in the 1992 presidential election. However, the IRS notified the church that if they did not engage in further violations of the IRS statute, their tax-exempt status would remain. Furthermore, in the few cases in which the IRS has fined churches, it has done so for activities of the church outside of the pulpit.

Here is the bottom line for pastors: no local church has ever lost its tax-exempt status or been fined by the IRS for sermons a pastor has preached.[21] Even when a group of thirty-seven pastors chose to challenge the constitutionality of the IRS prohibition against endorsing candidates in the 2008 presidential campaign by supporting Republican candidate John McCain from their pulpits, their actions were ignored by the Internal Revenue Service. Although I would not encourage pastors to officially endorse or oppose specific candidates for elected office from the pulpit, I would strongly urge pastors to preach their convictions about moral issues without being intimidated by those who would seek to muzzle God's prophets.

## ★ A Fear of Controversy ★

Pastors make easy targets for criticism, especially from church members. It's easy for laymen to tell their ministers not to be concerned with numbers and only concern themselves with the spiritual health of the congregation. Yet those very same laymen will be the first to call for the pastor's head if attendance and contributions start declining. Any true shepherd of a local congregation must be concerned about the spiritual, organizational, and fiscal health of his flock. After all, although the universal church will never go out of business, many local congregations have shut their doors because of diminishing attendance. No pastor wants to be the catalyst for killing his church.

As a pastor, I am very sympathetic with other pastors who are concerned about taking controversial stands that could send their congregants out the door and discourage new members from coming. For the first fifteen years of my pastoral ministry I rarely spoke about issues such as abortion or homosexuality from the pulpit, choosing instead to simply preach the Bible. I refused to encourage my members to vote in elections, much less provide them with any criteria for choosing candidates, rationalizing that government was powerless to effect any lasting change.

But thirteen years ago, I radically changed my beliefs and behaviors. A member in my church who worked in the local public library brought me two children's books promoting homosexuality, titled *Daddy's Roommate* and *Heather Has Two Mommies*.[22] You can probably figure out the plot of each book, told from a child's point of view. One page in *Daddy's Roommate* showed Daddy and his homosexual partner, Frank, in bed with these words: "Daddy and Frank sleep together."[23] The library employee asked me point-blank, "Pastor, what are you going to do about this?"

It just so happened that in my sermon series through the book of Genesis I had come that very week to Genesis 19: the story of Sodom and Gomorrah. My planned message on God's destruction of these cities included this principle: "We cannot afford to condone what God has condemned." By handing me these two books, this library employee was unknowingly forcing me to confront the strength of my convictions about refusing to condone what God has condemned.

On Thursday afternoon before my Sunday message, I called the head librarian, explained my concern about a children's book like *Daddy's Roommate* that promoted behavior (sodomy) that was illegal at the time in our state, that was condemned by the world's three major religions, and was responsible for the greatest epidemic in modern history (AIDS). I asked her to remove both of the books. She refused. The following Sunday morning I held up the books in the pulpit, explained my objection to them, and said to the congregation and television audience that I was not going to return the books to the library.

Thus began a two-year controversy that involved the local newspaper calling for me to be arrested and incarcerated and a federal lawsuit against our city. PBS filmed a documentary on the dispute that was dividing our town. For two years the Letters to the Editor section of the local paper was regularly filled with vitriolic letters from readers denouncing me and our church.

I wish I could report that our church exploded in growth during those twenty-four months because of the stand I took. It didn't happen. While only a handful of people left, relatively few new members came to the church during that time. After all, who wanted to join a church that was being labeled regularly as "judgmental" and was being blamed for dividing the entire community? Some of my closest friends and most valued staff members privately wondered whether my stand was worth the price the church was paying. "Think about all of the people who rightly or wrongly will never step foot in our church and have the opportunity to be saved because of what you have done," one leader lamented.

I recount my experience to you who are pastors only because I want you to know that I understand why you might be wary of taking bold stands on controversial issues. Although you may not feel called to "borrow" controversial books from your public library (I did pay for them through a fine), God has charged you with the responsibility to confront your culture with His Word. Preaching biblically based messages on controversial topics, encouraging and equipping your members to vote, and challenging laws that violate God's standard of righteousness are just some of the ways pastors can fulfill their role as prophet.

While such actions may not cost you your life, they may cost you your reputation, your security, and even your livelihood. Prophets and their messages have never been popular. As one writer notes:

> Noah's message from the steps going up to the Ark was *not* "Something good is going to happen to you!" Amos was *not* confronted by the high priest of Israel for proclaiming, "Confession is possession!" Jeremiah was *not* put into the pit for preaching, "I'm O.K., you're O.K." Daniel was *not* put into the lion's den for telling people, "Possibility thinking will move mountains!" John the Baptist was *not* forced to preach in the wilderness and eventually beheaded because he preached, "Smile, God loves you!" The two prophets of the tribulation will *not* be killed for preaching, "God is in his heaven and all is right with the world!"[24]

At the risk of offending some, allow me to be blunt. Pastors, you will likely not be persecuted or even criticized for opening a homeless shelter or encouraging your members to forsake materialism and give sacrificially to build water wells in Africa. Our culture will applaud you for such efforts because these actions fit the stereotype of what pastors are supposed to be doing. No one feels threatened as long as pastors stick to their major job assignment of being nice people who encourage other people to do nice things.

But a pastor who dares to point his finger in the face of unrighteousness and declare, "Thus saith the Lord" is going to become a target of criticism and persecution from without *and* from within the church. That reality is what motivated Paul to encourage Timothy to be prepared to "endure hardship" if he was faithful to "reprove, rebuke, [and] exhort" by confronting people inside and outside the church with the Word of God (2 Timothy 4:5, 2).

## ★ The Pastor as Evangelist ★

"Do the work of an evangelist," Paul reminded his pastoral protégé, Timothy (2 Timothy 4:5). I don't believe that Paul had in mind our idea of an evangelist, described by one person as a preacher traveling the country with five suits and five sermons. The word *evangelist* simply means "one who proclaims the good news of the gospel."

The final command Jesus gave His disciples was to go throughout the world and "make disciples" (Matthew 28:19). Bill Hybels has defined that mandate as "turning irreligious people into faithful followers of Jesus Christ."[25] Jesus Himself described a disciple as one who will "observe all things that I commanded you" (Matthew 28:20). In recent years many leaders have lamented that we have made numerous converts, but not many disciples. That is a valid concern. Far too many Christians have not grown in their relationship with God beyond their initial decision to trust in Christ for their salvation. To be a disciple means to imitate the actions and attitudes of Jesus Christ in every area of our life.

To make disciples requires that we first make converts, and we do that by doing the work of an evangelist—introducing unbelievers to the good news of Christ's death for our sins. That message is foundational to discipleship and is the "word of life" that the church is to "hold fast" in this dark world (Philippians 2:16).

No church will ever be more evangelistic than its pastor. That reality prompted Paul to exhort Timothy, the pastor of the church at Ephesus, to "do the work of an evangelist, fulfill your ministry" (2 Timothy 4:5). How can we pastors apply that first-century command in the twenty-first century?

## ★ Through Preaching ★

As we have already seen, our first duty as a pastor is to preach the Word. But exactly what "word" are we to proclaim? Paul answers that question in his letter to the Christians at Corinth:

> And when I came to you, brethren, I did not come with superiority of speech or of wisdom, proclaiming to you the testimony of God. For I determined to know nothing among you except Jesus Christ, and Him crucified. (1 Corinthians 2:1–2)

Paul is not suggesting that the only message he ever preached to the Corinthians concerned Jesus' death on the cross for our sins. When you read 1 Corinthians you will discover Paul taught about a number of topics: discipline in the church, divorce and remarriage, spiritual gifts, the role of women in the church, and the resurrection, to name just a few. What Paul is saying is that the good news of Christ's death for our sins was foundational to his preaching. Everything he taught was built upon that central truth. How can we pastors make sure that same message is central in ours as well?

First, we need to be sure that in every message we include some explanation of the gospel so that any unbeliever listening would know how to become a Christian. Charles Spurgeon, called the "prince of preachers," said that no matter what passage of Scripture he was in he always made a beeline to the cross. Admittedly, that is not always easy, but it is essential if we are going to fulfill our ministry as an evangelist.

Second, I would encourage every pastor to always challenge unbelievers who are listening to the sermon to make a decision to trust in Christ. As a Southern Baptist pastor I am often kidded by some of my friends from other denominations about extending invitations for people to come to the front of the church to publicly profess their faith in Christ. Yes, I realize that there are no examples of "walking the aisle" in the New Testament—mainly because there were no aisles to walk since the early church had no buildings for the first three hundred years of its history. But there is also no example in the New Testament of anyone preaching a sermon without asking the audience to render a decision about Jesus Christ.

Pastor, if your tradition is not one that encourages people to publicly indicate their decision to trust in Christ, you can always invite people to indicate their decision on a card or to meet with you or others after the service. The method of response is secondary to the necessity of calling for a response. The most famous evangelist of the nineteenth century, Dwight L. Moody, relates the tragic consequences of not encouraging an audience to make a decision about Christ from something that happened to him in the fall of 1871:

I intended to devote six nights to Christ's life. I had spent four Sunday nights on the subject and had followed him from the manger along through his life to his arrest and trial, and on the fifth Sunday night, October 8, I was preaching to the largest congregation I had ever had in Chicago, quite elated with my success. My text was "What shall I do then with Jesus which is called the Christ?" That night I made one of the biggest mistakes of my life. After preaching . . . with all the power that God had given me, urging Christ upon the people, I closed the sermon and said, "I wish you would take this text home with you and turn it over in your minds during the week, and next Sunday we will come to Calvary and the cross, and we will decide what we will do with Jesus of Nazareth."

At that moment, a firebell rang and Moody dismissed the meeting. That bell signaled the beginning of the Chicago Fire that killed 300 residents of Chicago and left 90,000 people homeless. Moody never had the opportunity to finish his series.

Years later he said, "I have never seen that congregation since. I have hard work to keep back the tears today . . . Twenty-two years have passed away . . . and I will never meet those people again until I meet them in another world. But I want to tell you one lesson I learned that night, which I have never forgotten, and that is, when I preach to press Christ upon the people then and there, I try to bring them to a decision on the spot. I would rather have [my] right hand cut off than give an audience a week to decide what to do with Jesus."[26]

## ★ Through Equipping ★

The pastor is to be an evangelist, but he is not to be the only evangelist in the church. My mentor for many years, Dr. Howard Hendricks, used to quote Bud Wilkinson's definition of football: "Twenty-two men on the field desperately in need of rest being cheered on by fifty thousand spectators in the stand desperately in need of exercise." Professor Hendricks would say, "That might make for exciting football, but it is a lousy way to run a church!" God never intended for the ministry of evangelism to be confined to the paid professionals. Instead, He wants every Christian to be in the game. Why?

The majority of non-Christians will never come through the doors of a church to hear about the saving power of Jesus Christ. That is why the primary strategy of the early church for spreading the gospel of Jesus Christ was not "come and hear" but "go and tell."

If we are serious about appearing as lights in the world, every Christian must be both willing and able to take the message of Christ from the church into our neighborhoods, schools, places of work, and relationships. Of course, such a strategy requires equipping every Christian so that he is able to share the message of Christ—and that is part of the pastor's responsibility:

> And He gave some as apostles, and some as prophets, and some as evangelists, and some as pastors and teachers, *for the equipping of the saints for the work of service,* to the building up of the body of Christ. (Ephesians 4:11–12; emphasis added)

Pastors are to equip their members (the saints) for the purpose of "building up of the body of Christ." The word *equip* originally referred to the loading up of a ship with supplies before it set out on a long journey. The primary role of the pastor is to provide his members with the supplies they need for the ministry of "building up of the body of Christ."

The word translated "building up" is a Greek word that referred to the building of a house. God asks us to partner with Him in constructing a spiritual temple for His glory that is composed of people, rather than stones (1 Peter 2:5). Whenever we lead someone to trust in Christ as Savior, we are adding another stone to God's temple. The temple God envisions is so large that it requires more workers than those who have been called by God to serve as pastors. God wants all Christians to be involved in this building project, and that requires pastors to equip their members for this project.

Our church offers a four-week training program several times a year for members on how to share their faith. Realizing that every member can't (or won't) commit to that length of time, I also occasionally devote a sermon to training our members on how to present the gospel to an unsaved person. One Sunday I gave everyone in the congregation an evangelistic booklet and explained how to use that booklet with a non-Christian. The result was that a number of Christians felt equipped to share the gospel message, and a few unbelievers listening to the presentation were saved!

## ★ Through Organizing ★

Read through the book of Acts, which chronicles the travels of the apostle Paul, and you discover very quickly that Paul was a man with a plan—a strategy for blanketing the world with the message of Christ. Occasionally Paul's plans were vetoed by God, such as the time the apostle wanted to go into Bithynia but God rerouted him to Macedonia so that the gospel would be preached for the first time to present-day Europe (Acts 16:6–9). However, the fact that Paul's plans were subject to God's sovereignty did not keep Paul from developing a strategy for spreading the gospel to as many people as possible.

Pastor, what is your strategy for taking the good news of Jesus Christ out of your church and into your community? If God has placed your church as a lampstand to illuminate Jesus Christ, what is your plan to maximize the unique opportunity you have to share the light of the gospel in this increasingly dark world?

Recently, I became convicted that while our church did a fabulous job of speaking to ourselves and even to other Christians in our city and in the world, we were making little measurable impact on the multitude of non-Christians who were living in our city. As I mentioned in chapter 1, I challenged our members to join The Pastor's Light Force by committing to pray for and develop a relationship with one non-Christian during a three-month period of time. Additionally, members of the Light Force committed to inviting that person to attend a special evangelistic service in our church in which Texas Rangers baseball star Josh Hamilton would share his Christian testimony.

Nearly one thousand members made the commitment to join me in this effort. Over the three-month period leading up to that special Sunday we trained the Light Force in how to develop a relationship with unbelievers, how to share the gospel with them, and how to follow up with those who trusted in Christ. During those three months we heard incredible stories about members who established relationships with unbelievers and some who were able to lead others to Christ before the big Sunday (and yes, we allowed that!). Many talked about a new energy they had gained from the realization that God had a greater purpose for their lives.

A number of our members who had not officially become a part of our group still invited guests to come on the designated Sunday. The result was that on that Sunday we experienced the largest recorded attendance in the history of our church. After I finished interviewing Josh, I gave a simple presentation of the gospel, giving people an opportunity to respond by indicating their decision to trust in Christ on a card we provided. That day 847 people indicated that they prayed to become a Christian! We spent the next weeks calling, visiting, and sending follow-up materials to each one who made that decision.

I am not suggesting that every church could or should adopt *our* plan. But every pastor and church should have a plan for reaching their communities with the message of Christ. The story is told that an angry man reportedly approached D. L. Moody, charging, "I don't care for your method of evangelism." Moody calmly replied, "I like my way of doing evangelism better than your way of not doing evangelism!" Pastor, what is your strategy for equipping the Christians God has entrusted to you to take the gospel into the community in which He has planted you and your church?

Fellow pastors, I especially encourage you to read this statement slowly and carefully . . . and then consider what implications it might have for your ministry:

> The preservation of our nation for the proclamation of the gospel depends upon the effectiveness of local congregations in fulfilling their mission. And the effectiveness of local congregations in fulfilling their mission depends upon pastors fulfilling their calling: as preachers, as prophets, and as evangelists.

# CHAPTER
## 6

## When Persecution Comes

**M**illions of people around the world have enjoyed the intriguing novels and insightful nonfiction books of Christian author Randy Alcorn. However, many readers are not familiar with his personal story that redirected his life and ministry. When he was twenty-two, Alcorn joined with another man to form the Good Shepherd Church in Boring, Oregon, a suburb of Portland. The church quickly grew into one of the largest churches in the city. Alcorn frequently spoke out against abortion and served on the board of a local pregnancy center. "The issue was consuming my mind and heart. When that light is turned on, you can't turn it off," Alcorn said years later.[1]

In January 1989, Alcorn asked his elders for permission to participate in local, peaceful protests at abortion clinics. The elders reluctantly acquiesced to their pastor's request. Alcorn and his fellow protesters marched in front of the abortion clinics, sometimes blocking access with their bodies. The abortion clinics fought back, pursuing every legal remedy at their disposal to keep their clinics open and protect the rights of the women who used them. Alcorn was arrested frequently. He recalls hearing one lawyer for an abortion clinic saying in court, "My clients have every bit as much right to perform abortions as McDonald's does to sell hamburgers." While true legally, Alcorn knew that under God's laws, murder was never permissible and so he continued his protests.

One of the clinics that Alcorn blocked sued him, followed by another clinic that eventually won a judgment for $8.2 million dollars against the pastor. Alcorn told the judge that he would pay any money that he legitimately owed, but his conscience would not allow him to turn over money to an abortion clinic that would be used to kill babies. When Alcorn discovered that the court would garnish one-fourth of his wages every pay period to help satisfy the judgment, Alcorn realized that his church was being placed in an untenable situation. If the congregation defied the court order, they would face possibly years of expensive litigation and turmoil. To prevent that from happening, Alcorn resigned as pastor and lived off his modest book royalties at that time.

However, Alcorn faced another challenge. He was still adamant that no portion of his book royalties be turned over to the abortion clinic. The only way to prevent the garnishment of his royalties was to work for minimum wage. Fortunately, frugality was already a way of life for the Alcorn family. Although his book sales have exploded during the last twenty years, Alcorn still lives in the same modest three-bedroom home and works for minimum wage (plus speaking honorariums) writing his best-selling books. He has not used an ATM or written a check since 1990.

Randy and his wife, Nanci, are quick to point out the many benefits that have accrued to their family because of this experience. "It would have been very difficult to leave the pastorate to become a writer and speaker. Suddenly I had no choice," Alcorn said in an interview with *Christianity Today*. Nanci refused to wallow in self-pity over their situation. However, after seeing one of their best friends and fellow abortion protesters spend nine months in jail after losing his job and home, Nanci observed, "The experience taught us to understand what it means to say, 'We won't always receive justice in this world.'"[2]

Any Christian who dares to take seriously the mandate to be salt and light in this world may not always receive justice but will almost always receive persecution. Such a guarantee comes from Jesus Christ. "In the world you have tribulation, but take courage; I have overcome the world," Jesus assured His followers (John 16:33). The apostle Paul who, before his conversion, had been an instrument of persecution against Christians, almost overnight became a target of persecution. In his second letter to the Corinthian Christians, Paul highlights some of the suffering he had endured because of his fearless proclamation of God's truth:

Five times I received from the Jews thirty-nine lashes. Three times I was beaten with rods, once I was stoned, three times I was shipwrecked, a night and a day I have spent in the deep. I have been on frequent journeys, in dangers from rivers, dangers from robbers, dangers from my countrymen, dangers from the Gentiles, dangers in the city, dangers in the wilderness, dangers on the sea, dangers among false brethren; I have been in labor and hardship, through many sleepless nights in hunger and thirst, often without food, in cold and exposure. (2 Corinthians 11:24–27)

Paul's experiences were not the exception but rather the rule for first-century believers. As the writer of Hebrews notes:

[Believers] were tortured, not accepting their release, so that they might obtain a better resurrection; and others experienced mockings and scourgings, yes, also chains and imprisonment. They were stoned, they were sawn in two, they were tempted, they were put to death with the sword; they went about in sheepskins, in goatskins, being destitute, afflicted, ill-treated (men of whom the world was not worthy), wandering in deserts and mountains and caves and holes in the ground. (Hebrews 11:35–38)

When reading passages like the ones above we try to assure ourselves that we will never have to endure such persecution because we live in a different time in history. Yet more Christians died as martyrs during the twentieth century alone than in all other centuries combined.[3] Indeed, the only reason we in the West feel immune to persecution is because of the self-created bubble in which we reside. American Christians, like Americans in general, are largely unaware of what is happening in the rest of the world. If you feel that statement is an exaggeration, consider that a National Geographic–Roper Public Affairs poll revealed that fewer than 3 in 10 young Americans ages 18-24 felt that it was absolutely necessary to know where the countries in the news are located.[4]

In spite of our ignorance of the world around us, at this very moment Christians around the globe are enduring severe persecution for their faith. Since 2003, Iraqi Christians have been frequent targets by Islamic extremists. In October 2008, more than a dozen Christians were killed in Mosul during a two-week period.[5] In Iran, authorities arrested seventy Christians over a two-and-a-half-week period of time in an effort to target grassroots Christian groups Iran describes as "hard-liners" who pose a threat to the Islamic faith.[6] In January 2011 a judge in Afghanistan told Shoaib Assadullah that if he did not renounce Christ within one week he would face up to twenty years in prison or even be sentenced to death.[7] In 2011, twenty-one Egyptian Christians lost their lives and nearly eighty were wounded in an attack on New Year's as they left a worship service. The attack was believed to be instigated by al-Qaeda militants who continually threaten Egyptian believers.[8]

Today, more Christians are imprisoned in China than in any other country in the world. Hundreds of thousands of believers are detained in work camps each year without a court order so that they can participate in a "reeducation through labor" program, as the Chinese call it. The only legal churches allowed by the Chinese government are those that are controlled by the government. Christians who meet in house churches not sanctioned by the government risk torture, imprisonment, and death.[9]

Philip Yancey describes a visit with Pastor Allen Yuan, who helped to found the house church movement in China during the Japanese occupation. Yuan, ninety years old at the time of his interview with Yancey, had spent twenty-two years in prison. He had been tortured and spent months in solitary confinement in a windowless cell. "I pulled the blankets over my head and prayed. For ten years no letters from my family got through. I had no Bible, but a few passages and psalms stayed with me," Yuan recounted. The pastor spent thirteen years of his sentence in China's most northern province. "It was a miracle! I had only a light jacket and in the freezing winter weather I never caught a cold or the flu. Not sick a single day!" Yuan testified.[10]

Pastor Yuan is convinced that persecution is not only inevitable but also profitable for believers. "We live in a time like the apostles. Christians here are persecuted, yes. But look at Hong Kong and Taiwan—they have prosperity, but they don't seek God. I tell you, I came out of that prison with faith stronger than I went in. Like Joseph, we don't know why we go through hard times until later, looking back. Think of it: we in China may soon have the largest Christian community in the world, and in an atheistic state that tried to stamp us out!"[11]

Christians experienced intense suffering for their faith during biblical times. Believers around the world have experienced and continue to experience persecution today. The Bible also predicts that during the final years before Jesus' return to earth, Christians will experience unprecedented hardship. The apostle John describes a large group of believers who will be slain during the time of the Tribulation:

When the Lamb broke the fifth seal, I saw underneath the altar the souls of those who had been slain because of the word of God, and because of the testimony which they had maintained. (Revelation 6:9)

The instigator of this intense, worldwide persecution of God's people will be a person called "the beast" or, as we refer to him today, Antichrist. The apostle John makes it clear that the primary target of Antichrist's fury will be God's people:

It was also given to him to make war with the saints and to overcome them, and authority over every tribe and people and tongue and nation was given to him. (Revelation 13:7)

In what way will Antichrist "make war with the saints"? One method of persecution will be by restricting the purchase of necessary goods and services to only those who worship Antichrist. This worldwide leader will have a lieutenant (commonly referred to in Scripture as "the false prophet") who will enforce the global mandate to worship Antichrist. This false prophet will require that every citizen in the world receive a mark of some kind that will demonstrate his or her allegiance to Antichrist and allow for the purchase of goods:

And he causes all, the small and the great, and the rich and the poor, and the free men and the slaves, to be given a mark on their right hand or on their forehead, and he provides that no one will be able to buy or to sell, except the one who has the mark, either the name of the beast or the number of his name. Here is wisdom. Let him who has understanding calculate the number of the beast, for the number is that of a man; and his number is six hundred and sixty-six. (Revelation 13:16–18)

Author Grant Jeffrey claims that the technology to essentially "barcode" human beings like we do toilet paper and books (like this one) is already available through radio frequency identification chips:

Many military intelligence agencies, government agencies, and large corporations have introduced sophisticated security systems requiring employees to wear a badge containing a radio frequency identification microchip. This RFID chip enables companies, agencies, and organizations to monitor the location and activity of every worker during every moment that he or she is on the premises. . . .

Using existing technology, the mark or number 666 can be implanted under the skin of every person using an RFID microchip. A powerful electronic scanner could detect the chip from a distance and reveal all your personal information, far more than your name, address, age, and marital status. While the implanted microchip and its information would be readable by a radio frequency scanner, a person would not know when or where his private information was being accessed—or who was accessing the information.[12]

Dr. David Jeremiah envisions the possibility of long lines of Christians waiting in a supermarket checkout line during the Tribulation, hoping and praying that somehow the barcode scanner will miraculously fail to notice that they do not have the necessary mark to allow for the purchase of food.[13] Such a terrifying thought is more than just a possibility; it is a certainty if we are to take John's vision of the end times seriously.

If we know that intense persecution was the experience of believers in biblical times, is the norm for Christians globally today, and is a certainty for believers living in the days immediately preceding Christ's return to earth, why should we be both surprised and unprepared when we experience persecution for our faith today?

Someone has said that there are three sermon topics that are guaranteed to draw a crowd at church: sex, the end times, and will there be sex in the end times? I regularly speak on the second subject and am amazed at the number of people who show up for a series on Bible prophecy. I have discovered that many come hoping against hope that I will declare whether we are living in the last days. I am the first to admit that I don't have any idea when Christ is going to return. In fact, Jesus Himself doesn't have a clue:

> But of that day and hour no one knows, not even the angels of heaven, nor the Son, but the Father alone. (Matthew 24:36)

How does God the Father know something that God the Son doesn't? That answer is far above my pay grade, but Jesus' statement should once and for all discourage serious students of the Bible from predicting the date of Christ's return.

Nevertheless, Jesus' words do reveal an often overlooked fact. God has marked a "day and hour" on His calendar when Christ is returning to reclaim this world for Himself. That means that every second that passes is moving us closer and closer to that event—an event that will be preceded by the intense persecution of believers.

## ★ What Is Persecution? ★

I think it is important to define terms here. By *persecution*, I mean negative consequences you experience because of your efforts to act as salt in restraining evil, or light in your efforts to share the gospel with others. Obviously, there is a spectrum of persecution that ranges from being excluded from a club because you are considered too opinionated to experiencing torture and death because of your refusal to recant your faith—and everything in between.

The degree to which you experience persecution as a believer is dependent upon two factors. First, the intensity of your conviction will determine the intensity of the persecution you face. The pastor who never addresses controversial subjects like abortion and homosexuality will never face ridicule by the media. The Christian student who refuses to challenge a professor's erroneous teaching will not have to worry about a lowered grade. A believer who decides not to offend his non-Christian parents by sharing the gospel with them will never risk their disapproval.

Second, the extent of the persecution you face is determined by the spiritual climate of the culture in which you live. As our culture increasingly loosens its ties to our nation's Christian heritage, we should expect growing hostility toward those who attempt to stem the tide of evil sweeping our land and continue to "[hold] fast the word of life" (Philippians 2:16) by insisting that Jesus Christ is God's exclusive provision for eternal life. If you are not convinced that the spiritual climate of our nation has become largely hostile toward Christianity, ask yourself how people—especially the media—would respond if the president of the United States made these remarks during a televised speech from the Oval Office:

> The general principles, on which the Fathers achieved independence, were . . . the general principles of Christianity. . . . I will avow, that I then believed, and now believe, that those general principles of Christianity, are as eternal and immutable, as the existence and attributes of God; and that those principles of liberty, are as unalterable as human nature.[14]

These words were originally spoken by John Adams, the second president of the United States. If the president uttered those words today there would be an outcry across the nation to begin impeachment hearings! Collectively, our country has increasingly disavowed its unique ties to Christianity.

Secularists would attribute the change in our nation's attitude toward Christian pronouncements from the White House to cultural enlightenment that has made us more sensitive to the different religious beliefs in our country and, therefore, more negative toward the elevation of one religion over another. Biblicists would argue that according to Romans 1 it is a cultural darkness, caused by people's rejection of truth, that makes them hostile toward the truth.

Regardless of the reason, it is obvious to the most casual observer that our culture is more hostile toward Christianity than any other time in our nation's history. Realizing that such negativity is more likely to increase rather than subside, it is only natural to expect an intensifying animosity toward those who dare confront the darkness of our culture with the light of God's truth.

## ★ Getting Ready ★

How should we respond to what I believe will be an escalating attack against Christians preceding Christ's return? The writer of Hebrews says that since we see "the day drawing near" Christians should be "encouraging one another" (Hebrews 10:25). One practical way to fulfill that command is by preparing fellow believers for the coming persecution. Keeping the following three words in mind is essential for fortifying yourself and others for the inevitable suffering that every genuine follower of Jesus Christ will experience.

## ★ Certain ★

The first documented case of Roman persecution against Christians as a group occurred under the reign of the emperor Nero in AD 64. On the night of June 18 a great fire erupted in Rome, destroying ten of the fourteen sections of the city. Many believed that Nero himself had set the fires. To deflect any blame for the catastrophe, Nero blamed the growing sect of Jesus followers known as Christians. The emperor devised the most heinous kinds of torture imaginable, including immersing Christians in wax and setting them on fire while still alive, serving as human torches to light his gardens. However, as in our culture, persecution against Christians did not happen suddenly but grew progressively. Nero was allowed to commit such atrocities against Christ followers because, as the pagan historian Tacitus notes, Christians were already "infamous for their abominations" within the general population.[15]

Most scholars agree that the apostle Peter wrote his first biblical letter one year before Nero began his empire-wide efforts to eradicate Christians from the face of the earth. Nevertheless, the undercurrent of hostility was already being felt by believers, so Peter tried to encourage them with these words:

> Beloved, do not be surprised at the fiery ordeal among you, which comes upon you for your testing, as though some strange thing were happening to you; but to the degree that you share the sufferings of Christ, keep on rejoicing, so that also at the revelation of His glory you may rejoice with exultation. (1 Peter 4:12–13)

"Do not be surprised . . . as though some strange thing were happening to you." I must confess those words always hit me between the eyes every time I read them, because they perfectly describe my knee-jerk reaction to the first hint of hardship that comes my way, especially when that difficulty is a direct consequence of my obedience to God: *God, are you asleep at the wheel? Don't you see what is happening to one of your most faithful servants? Lord, you've made a mistake. I'm supposed to be rewarded, not punished for following You. God, if this is how you treat your friends, no wonder You're having difficulty gaining a following!*

I'm not alone in my initial responses to suffering. When hit with hardships many Christians appear dazed and confused. They lose their spiritual equilibrium and stumble around in a stupor. They are shocked that obeying Christ has resulted in alienation from their friends, the loss of their job, or even the breakup of their marriage. The truth is we should be more surprised if we *aren't* suffering for our obedience to Christ. Peter says that persecution is the rule, rather than the exception, for those who have chosen to follow Christ.

Beyond surprise, we can become disillusioned with a God who would allow those of us He supposedly loves to endure severe suffering. After all, didn't the psalmist promise that in spite of the numerous adversaries that surround us, the Lord is a "shield about me" (Psalm 3:3)? Maybe God needs a bigger shield!

Yet looking at how God dealt with His own Son—His beloved Son—provides a different perspective on persecution. Suffering is not an unexpected detour in God's plan for our life but is actually a part of God's calling for us . . . just as it was for Jesus Christ.

For you have been called for this purpose, since Christ also suffered for you, leaving you an example for you to follow in His steps, WHO COMMITTED NO SIN, NOR WAS ANY DECEIT FOUND IN HIS MOUTH; and while being reviled, He did not revile in return;

while suffering, He uttered no threats, but kept entrusting Himself to Him who judges righteously. (1 Peter 2:21–23)

We are *called* to suffer? Frankly, that's the kind of call most of us would like to ignore or forward to someone else. Why would a loving God not only permit but actually plan for us to suffer? The answer to that question is found in the second word to keep in mind as we prepare for the coming persecution.

## ★ Profitable ★

While suffering may result in some temporary discomfort, the long-term gains can far exceed the short-term losses. On a personal level, the heat of persecution can fortify our faith. James, the half brother of Jesus, describes that phenomenon as he writes to a group of first-century believers who had been scattered across the Roman Empire because of their faith in Christ. They were bewildered over their circumstances, probably questioning the love or even the existence of the God they were following. Yet James begins his letter with a counterintuitive response to persecution:

Consider it all joy, my brethren, when you encounter various trials, knowing that the testing of your faith produces endurance. And let endurance have its perfect result, so that you may be perfect and complete, lacking in nothing. (James 1:2–4)

The Greek word translated "testing" (*dokimion*) means "approved." The word was used to describe the process of firing a piece of pottery in an oven. The potter's purpose was not to destroy the pottery but to strengthen it. If the item survived the fire, he would write the word *approved* on the bottom of the vessel. God, the Master Potter, is not interested in destroying your faith but in strengthening it. When He turns up the heat by allowing you to suffer for any number of reasons, He knows that He is actually strengthening your faith by driving you to Himself. As Warren Wiersbe says, when we are in the oven of God's testing, He always has His hand on the thermostat and His eye on the clock. He knows how long and how much![16]

Charles Spurgeon, the nineteenth-century preacher, endured more than his share of persecution from both unbelievers and believers alike for his strong stands. Spurgeon experienced regular bouts of depression, from which he eventually recovered. However, on one occasion, the depression lasted longer than normal. Concerned that he might descend further into his emotional abyss, his wife devised an unusual plan. She read this passage from Jesus' Sermon on the Mount that directly related to her husband's experience:

Blessed are you when people insult you and persecute you, and falsely say all kinds of evil against you because of Me. Rejoice and be glad, for your reward in heaven is great; for in the same way they persecuted the prophets who were before you. (Matthew 5:11–12)

Mrs. Spurgeon copied those words on a large piece of paper and taped it on the ceiling over their bed. When the pastor rolled over the next morning, he looked up and was at first startled by what he saw. He carefully read the words to himself, and then again out loud. Meditating on those words renewed Spurgeon's resolve to continue standing for the truth. As Chuck Swindoll observes, "When flat on our backs, the only way to look is up"![17] The corollary of that statement is that without suffering, we will not be forced to look up and experience God's strengthening of our faith.

Persecution is not only profitable for us individually, but it also benefits the Christian movement as a whole. Even the most cursory study of history reveals that persecution causes the church to flourish, while prosperity causes the church to retreat and wither away. The church father Tertullian (AD 160–230) reminded the governors of the Roman Empire of this fact in the conclusion of his *Apology*:

> Proceed in your career of cruelty, but do not suppose that you will thus accomplish your purpose of extinguishing the hated sect [the Christians]. We are like the grass, which grows the more luxuriantly the oftener it is mown. The blood of Christians is the seed of Christianity. Your philosophers taught men to despise pain and death by words; but how few their converts compared with those of the Christians, who teach by example! The very obstinacy for which you upbraid us is the great propagator of our doctrines. For who can behold it, and not inquire into the nature of that faith which inspires such supernatural courage? Who can inquire into that faith, and not embrace it, and not desire himself to undergo the same sufferings in order that he may thus secure a participation in the fullness of divine favour?[18]

Think for a moment about the experience of the early church, recorded in the book of Acts. Before He ascended to heaven, Jesus Christ told His followers what to expect next:

> But you will receive power when the Holy Spirit has come upon you; and you shall be My witnesses both in Jerusalem, and in all

Judea and Samaria, and even to the remotest part of the earth. (Acts 1:8)

Contrary to what many people assume, Jesus' words are not a command but a prophecy of what would happen to the apostles. After the Lord departed and the disciples received the Holy Spirit at Pentecost, they did not gather in a room, pull out a map, and strategize about how to take the gospel to "Judea and Samaria, and even to the remotest part of the earth." They would have been content to stay right at home in Jerusalem for the rest of their lives. Had that happened, the Christian movement would have been stillborn at its inception.

God knew that a good dose of persecution was exactly what the first church needed to get out of their holy huddles and scatter throughout the Roman Empire. And that's exactly what happened. After the stoning of Stephen, the first Christian martyr, believers fled from Jerusalem:

And on that day a great persecution began against the church in Jerusalem, and they were all scattered throughout the regions of Judea and Samaria. . . . Therefore, those who had been scattered went about preaching the word. (Acts 8:1, 4)

When you turn to Acts 12 you find that Herod Agrippa "laid hands on some who belonged to the church in order to mistreat them. And he had James the brother of John put to death with a sword" (Acts 12:1–2). How did the first-century believers respond to the growing persecution? It's no coincidence that the following chapter of Acts records the church taking the gospel message to "the remotest part of the earth." When the church is pressed, it expands.

Later in his life, the apostle Peter looked back on the beginning days of persecution and the resulting multiplication of the Christian faith, drawing the connection between the two:

> But even if you should suffer for the sake of righteousness, you are blessed. AND DO NOT FEAR THEIR INTIMIDATION, AND DO NOT BE TROUBLED, but sanctify Christ as Lord in your hearts, always being ready to make a defense to everyone who asks you to give an account for the hope that is in you, yet with gentleness and reverence. (1 Peter 3:14–15)

Nothing gives more credence to the Christian faith than the willingness of its followers to endure mistreatment. Don't be surprised when unbelievers ask those of you who are suffering to explain your faith, Peter advised. Instead, be prepared to explain "the hope that is in you."

The claim that the blood of Christians is the seed of Christianity is more than a nice theory; it is a verifiable reality. Consider the result of the torture and death of Stephen, the first Christian martyr:

> When they had driven him out of the city, they began stoning him; and the witnesses laid aside their robes at the feet of a young man named Saul. . . . Then falling on his knees, [Stephen] cried out with a loud voice, "Lord, do not hold this sin against them!" Having said this, he fell asleep. (Acts 7:58, 60)

Isn't it interesting that Saul, the most adamant persecutor of Christians at the time, was present and partly responsible for the murder of the first Christian martyr? While holding the coats of those throwing the stones, Saul witnessed Stephen's steadfast faith and heard his plea for God's forgiveness for his killers. It is more than coincidence that in the very next chapter of Acts, Christianity's greatest antagonist, Saul, was transformed into Christianity's greatest evangelist, the apostle Paul. Paul himself repeatedly referred to deaths like Stephen's as a catalyst for his conversion (Acts 22:4; 26:10).

Today the willingness of believers to endure mistreatment continues to be a powerful catalyst for the spread of Christianity. Soon Ok Lee was a prisoner in North Korea from 1987 until 1992. Although she was not a Christian at the time, she was imprisoned in North Korea with believers. She remembers hearing the Christians sing as they were being put to death. Not understanding their faith, she assumed they were insane. Because she was not allowed to communicate with other prisoners, Lee was never able to talk with the Christians, but she does recall hearing them say "amen." During the five years of her imprisonment, she never saw Christians recant their beliefs.

When those Christians refused to deny their faith, she remembers the guards becoming irate. She could not comprehend why those believers would not say "I do not believe" and spare themselves the horrendous torture they endured. Instead, the Christians would sing hymns as the beatings escalated. The guards would take them to the electric-treatment room. Lee says she never saw one Christian emerge from that room alive.

Eventually Lee escaped from prison to South Korea, where she became a Christian. By her own testimony, it was the enduring faith of those persecuted believers that implanted the seed of the gospel in her heart.[19]

## ★ Temporary ★

Last Christmas morning as we were planning to leave our house for a week-long vacation, my daughter awakened with excruciating pain in her abdomen. When she described her symptoms, I realized that she probably was suffering from a kidney stone—a diagnosis confirmed by a quick trip to the emergency room. I knew from personal experience the pain of these jagged calcium rocks stuck in the urinary tract. The only comfort I could provide her was the assurance that although her agony was horrendous, it was also temporary. Eventually, the pain would pass (literally!).

The apostle Peter wrote to Christians who were enduring very real pain for their faithfulness to Christ. Some were being imprisoned, others lost their livelihood, many were forced to choose between their faith and their families, and some were being executed in unimaginable ways. Peter never attempted to diminish the reality of their suffering, but instead he encouraged them through their ordeal with one small phrase:

> In this you greatly rejoice, even though now *for a little while*, if necessary, you have been distressed by various trials. (1 Peter 1:6; emphasis added)

"For a little while." Those are perhaps the most encouraging words to share with someone who is suffering, especially when that suffering is the result of his or her commitment to Christ. "I know this is hard, but this pain you feel will not last forever." Of course, one might naturally wonder, "How little is 'little'?" Does Pastor Yuan's twenty-two years in a Chinese prison camp qualify as "a little while"? Time is a matter of perspective. And so is suffering.

As we saw in the last section, the apostle Paul cataloged some of the persecution he experienced for the cause of Christ. But notice how Paul puts his suffering in perspective:

For *momentary, light affliction* is producing for us an eternal weight of glory far beyond all comparison, while we look not at the things which are seen, but at the things which are not seen; for the things which are seen are temporal, but the things which are not seen are eternal. (2 Corinthians 4:17–18; emphasis added)

Here is a guy who has been beaten within an inch of his life five different times, imprisoned, and shipwrecked. Yet he describes those experiences as "momentary, light affliction" as if they were nothing more than getting stuck in a slow line at the supermarket! Was Paul suffering from dementia? I don't think so. He is simply reminding us that the length ("momentary") and intensity ("light") of suffering on this earth are a matter of perspective.

For example, have you noticed how your perception of the passing of time changes the older you get? When you are a child, it seems that the school year will never end. As an adult, you cannot believe that another twelve months has passed so quickly. Someone has said life is like a roll of toilet paper: the closer you get to the end, the more quickly it goes! Actually, it's not the velocity that changes but only our perception of it. Pastor Yuan's twenty-two years in a Chinese prison camp must have seemed interminable at the time. After all, those years represented a large percentage of his entire existence on earth. But compared to eternity, those years were "momentary."

Paul also described his afflictions from persecution as "light." But again, that adjective is a matter of perspective. The apostle's suffering was "light" only when compared to the "eternal weight of glory."

Maybe this analogy will help you understand what Paul is communicating about suffering. Would you say that a two-thousand-pound concrete block was light or heavy? Most of us would answer "heavy"—unless we were comparing that one-ton block to a 747 jetliner. Compared to an airliner, the concrete block is light.

Paul is not in any way diminishing the pain many believers (like himself) experience from persecution. But when compared to the weight of God's rewards that believers will experience for eternity, such suffering can only be accurately described as light. As Teresa of Avila said, "In light of heaven, the worst suffering on earth, a life full of the most atrocious tortures on earth, will be seen to be no more serious than one night in an inconvenient hotel."[20]

Peter Lowe, the founder of a success seminar that bears his name, was once asked how he defined success. He responded, "First of all you have got to look at the long term. . . . I like to share with business people, 'If I could show you how to be a millionaire in thirty days would you like that?' They say, 'I'd love that.' 'Okay, you'll be a millionaire in thirty days, but only for one day, then you'll be bankrupt for the rest of your life.' Then it doesn't sound so good."[21] However, suppose that Lowe changed his offer. "You can be a millionaire for the rest of your life if you are willing to experience bankruptcy for one day." How many do you think would take him up on his offer?

Suffering, like success, is a matter of perspective. We hope we never have to choose between faithfulness to Christ and painful losses. But the stories of Christians from other generations and the experiences of fellow believers around the world tell us that we will probably not be exempt from such choices. I used to think that the martyrs of the Christian faith in days past and current heroes like Pastor Yuan were able to endure persecution because they possessed a greater threshold for pain than I. However, the more I read their stories, I realize that tolerance for pain is not the difference between them and most of us.

They had a different perspective. These heroes of the faith thoughtfully made their choice by weighing the temporary pain of persecution against the unending rewards from God. Using that scale, the choice was not difficult to make. And neither should it be for you . . . when persecution comes.

# CHAPTER
# 7

## Last-Days Living

I have shared with you my conviction that we are living in the last days. Why can I write this with such certainty? From an eschatological standpoint, the world is certainly closer (at least by two thousand years) to the Lord's return than when Christ and the writers of the New Testament began teaching about it. There are no outstanding prophecies that must be fulfilled before the great snatching away of believers to "meet the Lord in the air" (1 Thessalonians 4:17) can occur. It could happen before you finish this chapter.

Even if Jesus' return is still thousands of years away, you and I are certainly living in *our* last days. In thirty, forty, or fifty years, most of you reading this book will have died. Stop for a moment and do the math. Even if you live beyond the average life span to the age of eighty, go ahead and subtract your current age from eighty and see how many years you have left.

What if those remaining years pass as quickly as this past year? Perhaps you can now understand my assertion that you and I are living in our last days. Knowing that our days on earth are numbered and that we are headed for an eternity in heaven, to borrow from the late philosopher Francis Schaefer, "How should we then live?"

Many of Paul's letters, such as 1 and 2 Thessalonians, address the theme of last-days living. Some of the apostle's detractors, both then and now, try to discredit his writings by pointing out Paul's mistaken belief that the Lord would return in his lifetime. One skeptic writes:

> Paul himself showed that he was among those who awaited the imminent return of Christ. Yet, as the history of that era clearly shows, all was for naught. No messiah appeared. . . . The New Testament repeatedly says that the messiah was to appear in a very short time. Yet, mankind has waited for nearly 2000 years and nothing has occurred. . . . It is, indeed, unfortunate that millions of people still cling to the forlorn hope that somehow a messiah will arise to extract them from their predicament. How many years (2000, 10,000, 100,000) will it take for them to finally say, "We can only conclude that we are victims of a cruel hoax"?[1]

Yet a closer examination of Paul's writings reveals that while he never set a date for the Lord's return, he realized that the mere ticking of the clock was moving all of history closer to that climactic event:

Do this, knowing the time, that it is already the hour for you to awaken from sleep; for now salvation is nearer to us than when we believed. The night is almost gone, and the day is near. (Romans 13:11–12)

Paul had done the math. If there is a fixed date on God's calendar for His Son's return, then our ultimate deliverance (or as he terms it, "salvation") is closer today than it was when we were first saved, or even than it was this time yesterday. Imagine what the apostle would say if he were with us today: "Wake up and wipe the sleep away from your eyes. If the Lord's return was close two thousand years ago when I wrote to the Christians in Rome, think how much closer it is today!"

How should we conduct our lives knowing that the end is near, whether it is the end of the age or the end of our life? Knowing the eternal glory that awaits us, we should be optimistic, courageous, and productive!

Paul expressed the same idea to the Corinthian Christians. After spending an entire chapter painting a vivid picture of the kind of future that awaits Christians beyond the grave, Paul closes his discussion with a dose of practical exhortation:

Therefore, my beloved brethren, be steadfast, immovable, always abounding in the work of the Lord, knowing that your toil is not in vain in the Lord. (1 Corinthians 15:58)

As we watch the last glimmer of twilight fade to darkness in our culture, this single verse provides a needed road map for last-days living, utilizing three simple commands.

## ★ Be Hopeful ★

The billionaire investor Warren Buffet observed, "I have never seen Americans more fearful. It takes five minutes to become fearful, much more to regain confidence."[2] Certainly there is plenty to be apprehensive about. Just now I clicked on to a popular news website to see the glaring headline "Terrorist threat in U.S. is highest since 9/11."[3] Last night I heard an economist claim that because of the exploding budget deficit, no computer model could project a viable economy beyond the year 2037. If all of that were not enough, I just heard over the radio that I should not attempt to drive to work today because of a winter storm that is gripping our city. Dangerous black ice covers the streets, making travel potentially deadly.

Instead of being overwhelmed by the epidemic of fear that is so prevalent in these last days, Paul encourages us to be "steadfast" (*hedraios*). The word means "to be seated, firmly situated, or settled." I appreciated the value of this word earlier today when I ignored the meteorologists' warnings and ventured out to make a hospital visit. The gale-force winds that accompanied our Texas blizzard nearly knocked me down as I walked to the hospital entrance from the parking lot. Had I been sitting instead of walking, the winds would have had no effect on me. However, since sitting would not get me to my intended destination, I braced myself and moved forward slowly against the winds.

My persistence in moving forward to accomplish my task might be admirable, but it is not what Paul has in mind here. Rather than a sanctified call to brace ourselves against the howling winds of adversity, Paul is inviting us to actually enjoy our final days on earth. We can be "steadfast" rather than be overwhelmed by our circumstances because we know that our time on earth is quickly ticking away. And that knowledge provides security.

The Hebrew word for "security" comes from a root word that means "leisure." Eugene Peterson describes the kind of security God offers us as:

> ... the relaxed stance of one who knows that everything is all right because God is over us, with us and for us in Jesus Christ. It is the security of being at home in a history that has a cross at its center. It is the leisure of the person who knows that every moment of our existence is at the disposal of God, lived under the mercy of God.[4]

Instead of a braced, uphill ascent against the winds of opposition, a Christian's last days should be like a relaxed stroll on a spring day in the park.

Don't misunderstand what Paul is saying. He is not suggesting that we be lackadaisical in our attitude toward life. In other writings, Paul said that we are in a life-and-death battle against the forces of evil and that we should, therefore:

> Live life, then, with a due sense of responsibility, not as men who do not know the meaning of life but as those who do. Make the best use of your time, despite all the difficulties of these days. Don't be vague but firmly grasp what you know to be the will of God. (Ephesians 5:15–17 PHILLIPS)

By "seated" or "settled," the Word of God is referring to our inner emotions. In spite of the inevitable and increasing opposition we can expect in these last days, we can be settled in our spirits and relaxed in our stance, knowing that God is over us and that He is coming for us. The Bible calls the certainty of our rescue from this doomed planet "the blessed hope" (Titus 2:13).

Someone has said that a person is able to go forty days without food, eight days without water, four minutes without air, but he can only last a few seconds without hope. Without hope you are prone to become like Albert Camus, who wrote, "Why should I or anyone not commit suicide?"[5]

You could probably initially formulate a number of arguments against suicide, but those arguments ultimately fail if Camus's basic assumption is correct: there is no existence beyond the grave. The only hope that can keep us from being overwhelmed by the difficulties in this world is the knowledge that our Savior will one day deliver us to a better world.

For example, suppose you absolutely hate cold weather. The frigid temperature coupled with the lack of sunshine makes you dread winter. However, you work for a very generous employer who appreciates your contribution to the organization. Wanting to reward you for your productivity and to bolster your spirits during the inevitable winter climate that is approaching, your employer calls you in one October day and says, "I know how much you hate winter. So here's the deal I'm going to make with you. As soon as the temperature drops below 32 degrees and stays there for seven days in a row, I'm going to send you on a two-week, all-expense-paid vacation to Hawaii."

What would be your attitude when January rolls around? You would most likely be checking your smartphone hourly to see if the temperature had dropped to freezing. You might find yourself cursing the sun anytime it appeared from behind the clouds. Your hatred of heat would not be because of a sudden new affection you had for cold weather. You still dislike snow, ice, and gray skies. But you also realize that the sooner the temperature drops, the closer you are to your deliverance to the shores of Waikiki!

Jesus said, "I'm going to prepare a new world for you, and when it's ready, I'll return to pick you up." However, the destination Jesus has in mind is far superior to the blue waters and warm sands of Hawaii. And instead of having to return to frigid temperatures after a mere two weeks, your stay in the true paradise will be forever.

How do we know when we are getting close to departure time on God's eternal clock? Jesus says that instead of looking for falling temperatures, look for a heating up of world events: wars, famines, and persecution, to name a few. But rather than being discouraged over these events, we should be excited by them. Why?

> But when these things begin to take place, straighten up and lift up your heads, because your redemption [deliverance] is drawing near. (Luke 21:28)

Howard Hendricks likes to say that the dejected expressions that most believers wear on their faces would make them a perfect cover for the book of Lamentations! Pessimism is a poor advertisement for Christianity. Yet negativity is in vogue right now among believers. Every day I receive at least a half dozen forwarded e-mails from Christians that share a common gloom-and-doom theme: exploding deficits will have us standing in bread lines, illegal immigrants will rape and pillage our communities, and the current president will soon force us to worship Allah. It is almost as if Christians are trying to outdo each other with reasons we should be despondent.

Are you naturally drawn toward depressed people, or do you run for cover when you see them coming? Why would we expect non-Christians to be attracted to believers who have lost hope? Remember, Peter did not say, "Be ready to give an explanation to everyone who asks you for an account of the *dreariness* that is in you!"

The apostle says that we should not be surprised when people are attracted to us because of the hope that is in us, regardless of the negative circumstances happening around us. That is why it is imperative that we refuse to allow our emotions to be overwhelmed by threatening world events. Instead, we should remember that these increasingly dark days are a sign that our departure time for a better world is that much closer. And the hope that such a realization produces will act as a magnet, drawing unbelievers toward us and, more importantly, toward our message.

## ★ Be Courageous ★

Do you recall the story of the captain of an oil tanker who one night saw a light dead ahead of his ship? He directed his signalman to flash a message to the other ship: "Change course 10 degrees south."

The reply was quickly flashed back: "You change course 10 degrees north."

The captain was somewhat annoyed and sent a clarifying message: "I am the captain; change course 10 degrees south."

Back came the reply, "I am an able seaman. Change course 10 degrees north."

The captain, now infuriated, played his last card: "I am a 240,000-ton tanker; change course 10 degrees south!"

The final reply came back: "Change course 10 degrees north. I am a lighthouse!"

Compromise is the spirit of our age. After all, if there are no absolute truths that govern our world, shouldn't we be willing to engage in a little give and take with our beliefs? Why not sit down in an open dialogue with those who don't share our convictions and be willing to alter our position if they will alter theirs in return? Because, the apostle Paul says, those of us who are beacons of God's truth need to act like a lighthouse that cannot and will not be moved.

> Therefore, my beloved brethren, be steadfast, *immovable* . . . (1 Corinthians 15:58; emphasis added)

When our emotions are settled and at ease ("steadfast") by the knowledge that our departure is growing closer, we have every reason to courageously stand firm in our convictions. Knowing that the end is near instills boldness.

G. Campbell Morgan, one of the great expositors of Scripture, preached a message titled "The Fixed Heart in the Day of Frightfulness," describing the kind of courage that flows from a heart that is at peace:

> Men who are strong are always men who are fixed somewhere, who have a conviction from which they cannot be separated by argument, which cannot be changed, whatever the circumstances in which they live. Sometimes these men are very narrow, but they are wonderfully strong; they are singularly obstinate, but they are splendidly dependable. Consequently, we always know where to find these men. The fixed heart is the secret of courage. Courage is an affair of the heart; courage is the consciousness of the heart that is fixed . . . What, then, shall we do in the day of frightfulness? We shall do our duty; the thing that is nearest; the thing we have to do tomorrow morning. We will do that, and do it well; and do it cheerfully . . .What this nation needs, now just as much, and perhaps more, than anything else, is the multiplication of strong, quiet souls who are not afraid of evil tidings, even

though the zeppelins may be coming, and will not add to the panic that demoralizes, but will do their work.[6]

"Narrow . . . obstinate . . . dependable." Those are adjectives that have always characterized immovable men and women of faith. Consider the courage Daniel displayed while living under the reign of King Darius in Babylon. Because God had granted him favor in the eyes of this pagan monarch, Daniel had been promoted to serve as one of three presidents under the king. The country was organized into 120 regions, each having a "satrap" who governed the region and reported to one of the three presidents, who in turn reported to Darius. The satraps, envious of Daniel's meteoric rise to the top of Babylon's power structure, set a trap to ensure his quick demise.

Under the guise of patriotic fervor, the satraps approached Darius with a proposition to help unite their country:

All the commissioners of the kingdom, the prefects and the satraps, the high officials and the governors have consulted together that the king should establish a statute and enforce an injunction that anyone who makes a petition to any god or man besides you, O king, for thirty days, shall be cast into the lions' den. (Daniel 6:7)

These underlings knew their boss well enough to know how he would respond to such an idea. A suggestion rooted in blatant egotism, wrapped in the flag of nationalism, would be too much for Darius to resist. Darius signed the decree that would turn Daniel into dinner for the lions. How did Daniel react to the news about the new law? Like an immovable lighthouse:

> Now when Daniel knew that the document was signed, he entered his house (now in his roof chamber he had windows open toward Jerusalem); and he continued kneeling on his knees three times a day, praying and giving thanks before his God, as he had been doing previously. (Daniel 6:10)

Had Daniel been like most people he probably would have endlessly milked the messengers who brought the bad news with questions. "What was the exact wording of the decree the king signed?" "What was his demeanor?" "Did he saying anything about an exception for me?" Not Daniel. Instead of panicking, he began praying— with his windows *open* so that everyone might see him. This public display of intercession was not an attempt to tout his spirituality or flaunt his independence from the king. Daniel always prayed three times a day to God in front of any open window. Why would he change that now? Because of an edict from the king?

Daniel knew from experience that kings come and go. When he first arrived in Babylon, Nebuchadnezzar was on the throne. Like America today, Babylon was the only true superpower in the world. However, after a sleepless night ruined by a disturbing dream, King Nebuchadnezzar allowed Daniel to interpret his vision. God allowed the young prophet to peer down the corridor of history to see that the mighty power of Babylon would one day be usurped by another nation, and then another, and still another before the end of human history. Daniel concluded his interpretation of the vision with these words:

> In the days of those kings the God of heaven will set up a kingdom which will never be destroyed, and that kingdom will not be left for another people; it will crush and put an end to all these kingdoms, but it will itself endure forever. (Daniel 2:44)

Daniel lived to see Babylon defeated by the Medo-Persian Empire, led by King Darius, just as God had revealed to Daniel years earlier. But Daniel knew that Darius's days were also numbered. Instead of compromising his beliefs to accommodate the whims of transitory kings, Daniel chose to serve the Sovereign whose kingdom would endure forever. Daniel's insight about the future gave him the courage to be immovable in his convictions.

As we have seen, it is only a matter of time until believers in this country will experience genuine persecution for their faith. No, I'm not suggesting that overnight our government will begin executing those who profess Christ as their Savior. History reveals that persecution occurs more gradually. First, Christians are ostracized by others socially. Public ridicule of Christianity is both accepted and encouraged. Enemies of the faith convince the populace that the core beliefs of Christianity are detrimental to society. If you don't believe this effort is in full swing, ask yourself, when was the last time you saw an evangelical Christian portrayed in a positive way on television or in film?

Then, once the public has developed a genuine distaste for Christianity, government is free to begin limiting the rights of Christians while at the same time elevating the profile of other faiths, usually in the name of "multiculturalism." When Christians are socially ostracized and their rights are marginalized, it becomes much easier for government to target Christians with blatant persecution.

You may protest, "But America is different than any other country in history where persecution against believers has occurred. We have a Constitution that guarantees the right of religious freedom. We will never have to experience the kind of persecution other believers have faced." Are you sure?

As I type these words, Egypt is in turmoil over the ouster of its president. The news is filled with pictures of thousands of protesters in Cairo battling against government soldiers. Today it was announced that the government had "suspended" its constitution in order to preserve the peace. In our own country, we witnessed the suspension of the constitutional rights of Japanese Americans during World War II—all in the name of national security. There is a time coming when the constitutional rights of every American will be abolished. How can I make such a pronouncement with such certainty? As I explained in chapter 1, the books of Daniel and Revelation teach that one day the Constitution of the United States will be discarded.

As the prophet Daniel and the apostle John revealed, immediately before the return of Jesus Christ, a mighty government leader, commonly known as the Antichrist, will rule the world with an iron fist. Under his rule, all constitutional distinctions between nations will be abolished and all nations—including the United States of America—will give all authority to him in the name of world peace.

Every hour that passes moves us closer to that day when Christians living in the United States will lose all of their rights to worship freely. During those final seven years of history before the return of Jesus Christ, Christians will face a choice: obey the Antichrist or obey God and suffer the consequences.

However, we do not have to wait until the Constitution is revoked for persecution to begin. Instead, the continuing reinterpretation of the Constitution (especially the First Amendment) by the Supreme Court will provide sufficient authority for government to attack believers who defend the rights of the unborn, oppose same-sex marriages, exhibit their faith in the public square, and insist that Jesus Christ provides the only path to salvation. Fines, threats of losing tax-exempt status, and incarceration are just some of the consequences believers in America are already experiencing for refusing to compromise their convictions.

## ★ A Christian Response to Persecution ★

As we find ourselves living in the last days, we should not be surprised that more believers find themselves faced with the dilemma of choosing between obeying government and obeying God.

How should we respond when facing such a choice? In Acts 5, Luke records that Peter and the apostles were brought before the Jewish Sanhedrin, a ruling council of Jews that the Roman government empowered with the authority to take care of internal disputes among the Israelites. Acting under the authority of the Roman government, the High Priest reprimanded Peter for preaching the gospel of Christ:

> "We gave you strict orders not to continue teaching in this name [the name of Jesus], and yet, you have filled Jerusalem with your teaching and intend to bring this man's blood upon us." But Peter and the apostles answered, "We must obey God rather than men." (Acts 5:28–29)

Peter's response to these governing officials provides three important guidelines for how we should react when threatened with persecution for our convictions.

## ★ Pick Your Battles Carefully ★

Peter did not have to call a prayer meeting with the apostles to consider his answer to the officials because the apostle had already received his marching orders from Jesus Christ. "You shall be My witnesses," the Lord commanded the apostles shortly before He ascended into heaven (Acts 1:8). The clarity of Christ's command simplified the choice for Peter: obey Christ or obey the government. What other alternative did Peter have?

Similarly, when ordered to keep silent about our faith in Christ, we have no choice but to disobey human authorities. Christ's command to us is unmistakably clear. However, other times we do have a choice. Not every government law that carries religious overtones should be disobeyed. For example, recently the mayor of our city, who is also a member of our church, announced he is running for the United States Senate. He is not only a gifted leader but a genuine follower of Christ. I plan to do everything I can to support his candidacy. However, the government has said that there are some things I can't do or our church will lose its tax-exempt status. I am prohibited from using any church resources to support his campaign. I cannot stand in the pulpit and give a church endorsement for him.

Now, I could violate those restrictions, claiming, "We must obey God rather than men." However, where in Scripture does God explicitly command a church to support the candidacy of a politician? If my actions resulted in the loss of our church's tax-exempt status, I could not claim I was being persecuted for my faith. Instead, I would be persecuted for my lack of good judgment.

Christians who refuse to pay income tax because they object to how the money is used, believers who refuse to serve on a jury because they are required to take an oath, or Christians who refuse to respect trespassing laws when engaging in abortion protests should not claim they are being "persecuted for the sake of righteousness" (Matthew 5:10). Instead, they are being punished for failing to "render to Caesar the things that are Caesar's" (Mark 12:17). When we decide to engage in civil disobedience and defy human authority, it is important that our choice be based on clear biblical commands or principles.

### ★ Demonstrate Respect When You Disobey ★

When Daniel arrived in Babylon as a teenager, he was immediately confronted with a test of his allegiance to God. Daniel was singled out by King Nebuchadnezzar for his intelligence, discernment, and good looks to be part of an elite group of Hebrews who would serve the king's court—much like the White House Fellows program today that chooses exceptional young adults to serve the president of the United States. Part of Daniel's training program for this prestigious position required that he eat the king's choice foods and drink from his expensive collection of wine. The only problem was that such a diet violated the Mosaic law.

How did Daniel respond to the edict? He could have stormed into to the palace and said to Nebuchadnezzar, "You pagan king! I can't believe you would suggest that a holy man such as I defile himself by breaking God's law." Had he done so, he doubtlessly would have been the first Hebrew martyr in Babylon! While that distinction might have been admirable, Daniel would have forfeited the ministry that God had planned for him in Babylon for the next seventy years.

Fortunately, Daniel chose to display some of the wisdom and discernment that had made the king notice him in the first place. Daniel demonstrated his respect for the king's office by refusing to speak to him directly. Instead, Daniel approached the commander of the officials with an alternative suggestion that would achieve the king's ultimate goal. The commander acquiesced, the king's objective was fulfilled, Daniel's stock rose, and his convictions were not violated.

Peter demonstrated the same respect before the Sanhedrin officials when he was ordered to stop preaching. You don't read the apostle saying, "Why would I submit myself to a bunch of Christ-killers? Go jump in the lake of Galilee!" He refused to intimidate them with a "God is going to get even with you for trying to muzzle me" threat. Instead, he firmly and respectfully said, "We must obey God rather than men." Peter was emulating the response of Jesus Christ about whom he would later write, "And while being reviled, He did not revile in return; while suffering, He uttered no threats, but kept entrusting Himself to Him who judges righteously" (1 Peter 2:23).

In these last days, Christians will increasingly be challenged to courageously stand firm against those who deliberately—or sometimes innocently—attempt to abrogate our constitutional rights and our biblical mandate to spread the message of Jesus Christ. But in doing so, we don't have to act like jerks!

When my oldest daughter was in grade school, she came home one day and told me about a friend who was stopped by the principal for passing out water bottles labeled with John 4:14: "Whoever drinks of the water that I will give him shall never thirst." The principal, who was a committed Christian himself, told the girl that passing out the bottles violated the separation of church and state. My daughter asked, "Dad, can he do that?" "No," I explained. "He doesn't understand the First Amendment of the Constitution, which guarantees our right to express our faith." I decided that for the sake of the gospel, as well as a demonstration to my own daughter of standing up for truth, I needed to call the principal. I first called my friend Kelly Shackleford of the Liberty Legal Institute, which fearlessly champions the rights of Christians against overzealous secularists, to get some of the latest court rulings about this issue.

Once armed with the facts, I called the principal. First, I expressed my appreciation for all he had done for my daughters. I then acknowledged the difficult spot he was in as a Christian principal in a public school. Finally, I explained that while he probably thought he was doing his job in prohibiting the distribution of the water bottles, he was actually violating her rights—something I was sure he would not want to do. He thanked me for making him aware of the facts and reversed his position.

I realize this incident does not qualify as a landmark legal victory. However, in one small corner of West Texas, a little girl's constitutional rights were preserved and her efforts to spread the gospel were unfettered by a firm but courteous stand for truth. Think what would happen if every follower of Christ around the world would graciously but boldly push back against attempts to neutralize Christianity's influence on our culture. Too many Christians equate politeness with inaction and activism with rudeness. The result? We have unnecessarily ceded too much territory to the enemy by our polite silence.

## ★ Be Prepared to Suffer the Consequences for Disobedience ★

I am amazed when Christians boldly stand up for their convictions and then act surprised when they are punished for their actions!

Displaying courage does not exempt you from persecution. Consider the experience of civil rights leader and pastor Dr. Martin Luther King Jr.

Dr. King penned his famous "Letter from Birmingham Jail" while incarcerated for his nonviolent protest against the segregationist policies of downtown retailers. He wrote his letter in response to eight white clergymen who criticized King for his acts of civil disobedience, saying that the issue should be fought in the courts, not in the streets. In his response to those ministers, King wrote:

> One may well ask: "How can you advocate breaking some laws and obeying others?" The answer lies in the fact that there are two types of laws: just and unjust. I would be the first to advocate obeying just laws. One has not only a legal but a moral responsibility to obey just laws. Conversely, one has a moral responsibility to disobey unjust laws. I would agree with St. Augustine that "an unjust law is no law at all." Now what is the difference between the two? . . . A just law is a man made code that squares with the moral law or the law of God. An unjust law is a code that is out of harmony with the moral law.[7]

King firmly believed that laws codifying racial discrimination contradicted the moral law of God and therefore should be disobeyed. Whether you agree with King or not, you have to admire his courage to follow his convictions. King was not surprised that his stand against man-made laws landed him in jail. He did not complain about the injustice of a minister of the gospel having to do jail time for standing up for the rights of others. Martin Luther King Jr. understood that civil disobedience resulted in painful consequences.

I feel an affinity with Dr. King's experience because of something that happened to me a few years ago. When I refused to return two children's books promoting homosexuality to the local library, the editor of our local newspaper reminded his readers that Christians who violate the law need to be prepared to suffer the consequences of civil disobedience.[8]

That is one part of the editorial with which I completely agreed! Christians should not expect government authorities to break into a standing ovation when we defy their edicts by saying, "Here I stand. I shall not be moved."

Believers are rarely spared from experiencing the consequences of civil disobedience. After all, Daniel did end up spending the night in a den of lions for his refusal to obey Darius's command. Peter and the other apostles were beaten for their refusal to stop preaching the gospel of Christ. Jesus Christ was crucified for His unwillingness to submit to the Jewish and Roman authorities' demand that He deny His deity. And none of them complained about their punishment. In fact, notice the reaction of Peter and the apostles to the harsh beating they endured when they refused to stop preaching the gospel:

> . . . they flogged them and ordered them not to speak in the name of Jesus, and then released them. So they went on their way from the presence of the Council, *rejoicing* that they had been considered worthy to suffer shame for His name. (Acts 5:40–41; emphasis added)

Remember your parents' admonition, "No one likes a crybaby"? Nobody likes a crying, complaining Christian either. One reason for the exponential, explosive growth of Christianity in the first century was the supernatural response of believers to persecution. Instead of whining about their punishment, the apostles were grateful for the privilege of enduring mistreatment for the cause of Christ.

## ★ Be Productive ★

Paul closes his admonition for last-days living by encouraging the Corinthians to be "always abounding in the work of the Lord, knowing that your toil is not in vain in the Lord" (1 Corinthians 15:58). The word translated "abounding" (*perissueo*) pictures a river that overflows its banks. To "abound" means to exceed the boundaries or requirements by doing more than what is expected. The apostle is saying that the knowledge of Christ's imminent return and our resurrection should motivate us to turn on the afterburners in our work for God.

My most productive day at work in the entire year is the day before I leave on a vacation. As departure time approaches, I feel pressed to make sure that I plan for every possible contingency while I'm away. The extra motivation that comes from knowing two weeks of leisure are just around the corner provides me with extra energy to plow through the piles of paper on my desk that have been mounting for days. There is something about an upcoming journey that necessitates and motivates us to work especially hard.

The certainty that we are living in America's last days (or, at least, *our* last days) should not paralyze us with fear but energize us to pour our time and resources into expanding God's kingdom. Paul's imagery of an overflowing river provides three practical implications for what it means to be productive in these last days.

## ★ Proactive Living ★

I used to live on the border between Texas and Oklahoma. The two states were separated by the Red River, which most of the time was more like the Red riverbed. It was a pitiful excuse for a river. In all the times I drove over the "river" on my way to Oklahoma, I was never forced to abandon my car or alter my route because of what was mostly a swamp. However, whenever a river does overflow its banks (as the mighty Mississippi did recently), everyone living in its path is forced to abandon their location and run toward higher ground.

God's plan for these last days is for the church to put the world on the run, and not vice versa. Do you recall Jesus' words about the church in the days preceding His return?

Upon this rock I will build My church; and the gates of Hades will not overpower it. (Matthew 16:18)

Contrary to what many Christians believe about this verse, Jesus does not describe the church as hiding behind the gates, trying to survive Satan's battering ram. Just the opposite. Jesus pictures Satan and his forces of darkness cowering in fear behind the gates of their kingdom, attempting to fend off the invading church as we reclaim the world that the devil and his demons have taken hostage. The fortress Satan has erected is formidable, but it is no match for the spiritual firepower of Jesus and His followers.

Those of us living in the age immediately preceding the return of Jesus Christ represent the first wave of forces God has sent to infiltrate this world before our Commander returns for the final assault and reclamation of what is rightfully His. Instead of hunkering down and holding on until the Lord rescues us from this chaotic world,

God is calling us to go on the offensive by aggressively pushing back against evil and proactively expanding God's kingdom. Every day you live you have the opportunity to strike a blow against Satan's kingdom and pave the way for Christ's coming kingdom:

- Every time you lead someone to a saving faith in Christ, you have rescued someone from the enemy's camp and released Satan's grip on this world by just a little more.
- Every time you speak an affirming word to another Christian, you encourage one of our own troops, giving him strength to continue the fight.
- Every time you publicly credit God for something He has done for you, you refute the enemy's lie that there is no God and thereby break the spell he has cast over his captives.
- Every time you refuse to surrender an area of your life to Satan, you drive another stake in his plan and throw him into chaos.

Just as an overflowing river affects everything in its path, followers of Christ are to act offensively and put Satan and his minions on the run by salting this decaying world with righteousness and illuminating this darkened planet with the gospel.

### ★ Continuous Living ★

Paul says that we are to be "*always* abounding" in the work of the Lord. I believe that the single greatest roadblock to fulfilling this command is one of the most worshipped concepts in America: retirement.

The idea behind retirement is that you work as hard as you can for the first forty years of your adult life so that you can spend the final twenty years of your life waking up every morning asking yourself, "What can I do to entertain myself today?" Someone described retirement this way:

Since I retired from life's competition
Each day is filled with complete repetition
I get up each morning and dust off my wits
Go pick up the paper and read the obits
If my name isn't there, I know I'm not dead
So I get a good breakfast and go back to bed.[9]

God never intended for you to spend the final years of your life chasing a little white ball around a golf course or traveling the country in a Winnebago! A life that is focused on pleasure and leisure is one that is destined for spiritual atrophy and destruction. Jesus described people whose love for God is "choked with worries and riches and pleasures of this life" (Luke 8:14). It has been my experience as a pastor that many Christians who exchange a life of working for a life of leisure also "retire" from spending time in God's Word, praying, attending worship regularly, and serving others.

Retirement is a completely unbiblical concept. I challenge you to find one of God's servants in either the Old or New Testament who, after reaching a certain age, traded in his ministry for a pension check. Although you may not continue working at your present job until you die, God never intends for you to quit living a productive life. Even if you choose or are forced to retire from your vocation, Paul says that you and I are to be "always abounding in the work of the Lord" (1 Corinthians 15:58).

In his book *This One Thing I Do,* Franklin Graham relates the story of Charles McCoy, who pastored a Baptist church in Oyster Bay, New York. At age seventy-two, McCoy was required by his denomination to retire (using that ridiculous policy, Moses would have been disqualified from becoming the leader of the Exodus at age eighty!). McCoy was understandably depressed. "I just lay on my bed thinking that my life's over and I haven't really done anything yet. I've been pastor of this church for so many years and nobody really wants me much—what have I done for Christ?"

The following week he met a pastor from India and impulsively asked him to preach in his church. After the service, the Indian pastor invited McCoy to come preach for him in India. McCoy explained he was being forced to retire because of his age and was planning to move to a retirement home in Florida. However, the Indian pastor explained that in his country, men with white hair were respected. McCoy prayed about it and finally accepted the invitation. He sold or gave away most of his belongings, except for those that would fit into a trunk. He booked a one-way ticket to India, never having traveled out of the United States before.

Upon his arrival in Bombay, McCoy discovered that his trunk containing his belongings had been lost. All he had were the clothes he was wearing, his passport, wallet, and the address of some missionaries in Bombay he had clipped from a magazine. He boarded a bus to visit the missionaries. While on the bus, both his wallet and passport were stolen! When he finally arrived at the missionaries' home, they had no idea who he was. Furthermore, McCoy discovered that the Indian pastor who had invited him was back in the United States and had no plans to return to India!

But McCoy believed God had led him to India and refused to give up. He decided to make an appointment to see the mayor of

Bombay. Miraculously the mayor granted him an appointment, and upon seeing his business card listing his various degrees, he invited McCoy to preach to some of Bombay's highest officials. That preaching assignment began a sixteen-year ministry for Charles McCoy. Before he died at age eighty-eight, McCoy traveled the world preaching the gospel of Jesus Christ, never having more than enough money in his pocket to get him to his next destination.

Charles McCoy died in a hotel in Calcutta one afternoon as he prepared to preach that evening. Today, there is a church in Calcutta and a growing group of Christians in Hong Kong because this elderly servant of God refused to retire and instead was "always abounding in the work of the Lord."[10]

## ★ Strategic Living ★

Randy Alcorn uses a simple illustration to help his audience gain a perspective on life. He invites people to take a sheet of white paper and put a dot in the center. He then tells his audience to draw a line from the dot to the edge of the page. The dot represents the seventy or eighty years of life we have here on earth. The line represents eternity. "Right now we are living *in* the dot. But what are we living *for*? ... The person with perspective lives for the line.... The person who lives for the dot lives for treasures on earth that end up in junkyards. The person who lives for the line lives for treasures in heaven that will never end."[11]

Contrary to what some might believe, the apostle Paul was not a sadomasochist who enjoyed beatings and savored the prospect of being beheaded for his faith. So why did he willingly subject himself to such harsh treatment? Because he understood that living for the line was a much better investment, with a much longer payout, than living for the dot. As he approached his death, Paul explained his rationale for surrendering a life of comfort for a life of horrendous suffering:

> For I am already being poured out as a drink offering, and the time of my departure has come. I have fought the good fight, I have finished the course, I have kept the faith; in the future there is laid up for me the crown of righteousness, which the Lord, the righteous Judge, will award to me on that day; and not only to me, but also to all who have loved His appearing. (2 Timothy 4:6–8)

Paul doesn't say, "I'm investing my life to the point of death in God's work but not expecting anything in return." Paul was eagerly anticipating an eternal payback for the investment he had made of his life—a dividend that God would award to Paul, as well as to everyone who had chosen to live for the line, rather than the dot.

Paul reminds the Corinthians of the future reward in the final phrase of 1 Corinthians 15:58:

> Therefore, my beloved brethren, be steadfast, immovable, always abounding in the work of the Lord, *knowing that your toil is not in vain in the Lord.*

"God is not asking you to work overtime in this life for nothing," Paul assures us. "There is a payoff coming beyond your comprehension!" Someone illustrated the magnitude of that reward in an article I read years ago.

Suppose that you were alive when Jesus was born. When you heard the news you said to yourself, "You know, I think this baby is going places and I want to invest in his ministry." So you invested $1 in Jesus, Inc.—a business built on the life of Jesus Christ. Now let's assume that you never invested another dollar in Jesus, Inc., but that $1 investment yielded a 6 percent return every year. Can you guess how much that $1 investment would be worth two thousand years later if it compounded at 6 percent a year? 720 quadrillion dollars!

The problem with most of our investments is that we don't have a long enough time horizon. We invest our time or resources for ten, twenty, or thirty years in material things that will ultimately be stolen, lost, forgotten, worn out, or left behind when we die. But the wise person invests for eternity in God's kingdom, which will never be stolen, lost, forgotten, worn out, or left behind.

Although you and I were not alive when Christ was born to make that initial $1 investment, we are alive now and will live for the next two thousand, two million, and two trillion years. God invites you to invest your time and resources in His kingdom and receive a dividend that is "imperishable and undefiled and will not fade away, reserved in heaven for you" (1 Peter 1:4).

Let me introduce you to a man who understands the value of strategic investing. Andy Horner is a member of my church and founder of Premier Designs, a direct sales company that sells beautiful jewelry through forty thousand associates around the world. When Andy was sixty, he and his wife, Joan, decided to retire from another direct sales organization.

Through a series of confirming signs, God led Andy and Joan Horner to begin Premier Designs. The primary purpose for Premier Designs would be the support of Christian ministries in America and around the world. They purposed not just to give a percentage of their profits away, but to invest *all* their profits in Christian ministries. During the past twenty-seven years, Andy, his son Tim, and Premier Designs have given tens of millions of dollars to support missionaries and Christian organizations around the world.

Andy could have invested his profits in jet airplanes and luxurious mansions in every corner of the globe. With the money he and his family have earned, they could have enjoyed a luxurious, stress-free life. But the word *retirement* was not in Andy's dictionary. "Heaven is God's retirement center, and it is a lot more plush than Palm Springs or Sarasota. I wasn't about to look for shells in the morning on the beach and then play golf all day until a favorite TV sitcom came on that night. I knew God wanted me to change direction, not retire, and to accomplish a whole new mission," Andy said.[12]

Andy Horner is now eighty-seven years old. The other night I drove him home after a late church building committee meeting. He was to leave the next morning at 5 a.m. for a mission trip to Argentina! As I drove along the highway he shared with me a conviction he had about a project our church should be involved in. Then he said, "Now, Pastor, don't worry about the money. I'll provide the funding. It is so exciting to be able to make money and give it away to God's work!" Andy Horner is a man committed to spending his last years "abounding in the work of the Lord."

### ★ How Are You Responding to These Last Days? ★

What about you? As you find yourself in the twilight of earth's history—or at least of your own existence—how are you responding to these last days? Are you allowing the daily headlines or cable news pundits to paralyze you with fear? Are you depending on a politician or political movement to reverse the downward spiral of our nation? Or are you trying to ignore all the chaos and simply take care of yourself and your family until the end comes?

God has left you here at this critical time in history for a greater purpose than simply eking out a living and trying to survive the unexpected challenges life throws at you every day. God has enlisted you to become part of an offensive force with a specific mission. You and I represent the first wave of attack God has sent to infiltrate this enemy-controlled world and soften it up before our Commander returns for the ultimate reclamation of what is rightfully His.

The strategy for victory is twofold. God has called and empowered you to stand up and push back against evil and, at the same time, to illuminate the world with the eternal Light of Jesus Christ. As you witness the twilight turning to darkness, the need and the opportunity for you to do both have never been greater.

And remember, nighttime never lasts forever.

# FOR FURTHER REFLECTION

## CHAPTER 1: The Beginning of the End

1. Do you agree or disagree with the author's premise that America's collapse is inevitable? Why or why not?
2. Of the three "explosions" that have weakened our nation's spiritual infrastructure, which do you think is most serious? Why?
3. Most Bible scholars agree that America is not referenced in the book of Revelation. Why do you think that is?
4. Should government give preferential treatment to Christianity? Suppose that you had a choice between having representatives of Christianity, Judaism, and Islam voice a prayer at graduation on a rotating basis each year, or having no prayer at all. Which would you choose? Why?
5. Do you believe that God will condemn America for its tolerance of other faiths as He did Israel? Why or why not?
6. Do you believe that abortion is ever justified? What about cases that involve rape, incest, or the protection of the mother's life? Should Christians be willing to compromise on this issue in order to outlaw most abortions, or should they refuse to support legislation that allows for abortions in any circumstances?
7. Since conservatives typically believe in limited government, why should they attempt to outlaw homosexual marriage? Should homosexual acts between adults be outlawed? If your answer is yes, should government also outlaw adultery and premarital sex? Why or why not?

## CHAPTER 2: When a Nation Implodes

1. What role should Christians play in trying to change the culture?
2. How would you respond to the comment, "You can't legislate morality"?

3. Do you agree with the author's premise that Christians can "buy more time" for our nation and actually delay God's judgment upon our country? Why or why not?
4. Which is easier for a church to focus on: pushing back against evil ("salt") or sharing the gospel of Christ ("light")? Why?
5. Is the church you attend more focused on being "salt" or "light"? Which focus is most important for a church? Why?
6. What is your personal strategy for sharing Christ with other people? What could you do to become more intentional in that focus?
7. Why do you think Christians are reluctant to become actively involved in standing up against evil in our culture? What are some practical ways you could act as "salt" in your sphere of influence?

## CHAPTER 3: The Most Misunderstood Word in America

1. Why do you think tolerance is so exalted in our culture today?
2. Do you agree with the way the author defines tolerance? Why or why not?
3. Why do you think Christians have embraced what the author terms "pseudotolerance"?
4. Which aspect of "true tolerance" do you think Christians have most difficulty accepting: permitting different points of view with which they disagree or showing respect to the person with whom they disagree?
5. Are conservative Christians as intolerant as their critics claim? What, if anything, do you think Christians should do to change their image?

6. The author demonstrates that our Founding Fathers displayed a strong preference for Christianity while being tolerant of other religious beliefs. Do you think it is preferable or possible for our government to attempt that same balance today? Why or why not?

7. How has this chapter changed your understanding of tolerance? What changes could you make in your life to demonstrate true tolerance?

## CHAPTER 4: How a Christian Should Vote

1. Why do you think so many Christians fail to vote? Should churches actively promote voter registration? What are the dangers of doing so?

2. Should Christians attempt to exert control over the behavior of non-Christians in society? Why or why not?

3. How important is a candidate's religious faith to you? How can voters determine whether a candidate is a believer or not?

4. Would you ever vote for a Muslim for political office? What about an atheist? Why or why not?

5. Should an elected official allow his personal religious beliefs to affect his policies? Should a judge ever allow his personal religious beliefs to affect his ruling? Why or why not?

6. What controversial political issues do you believe the Bible clearly addresses? On what controversial issues do you believe Christians could legitimately disagree?

7. How would you respond to a Christian who said, "We don't need to be involved in the political process. After all, the Bible says 'our citizenship is in heaven'"?

## CHAPTER 5: For Pastors Only

1. Do you agree with the author's assertion that many Christians have devalued the importance of the local church? If so, why?

2. Of the various functions of the local church, which do you think is most important? Why?

3. Do you agree or disagree with the belief that pastors are no more "called by God" to their vocation than a plumber is to his vocation? Why or why not?

4. Do you agree that no church will fulfill its mission without its pastor fulfilling his calling as preacher, prophet, and evangelist? Why or why not?

5. Which of the three roles of the pastor (preacher, prophet, evangelist) do you think pastors find most difficult? Which do they find easiest? Why? What do you think laymen should do to encourage their pastor to fulfill each of these roles?

6. Suppose two candidates were running for mayor of your city: a strong Christian and an openly gay unbeliever. Should your pastor encourage the congregation to support the Christian candidate or should he remain quiet? Why?

7. What priority should evangelism have in a church? On a scale of 1 to 10, how effective is your church in sharing the gospel with unbelievers in your community? In what practical ways could your church improve its evangelistic outreach into your community?

## CHAPTER 6: When Persecution Comes

1. Do you believe Christians in America will ever suffer the same kind of persecution for their faith that other believers around the world have experienced? Why or why not?

2. Why do you think God has spared believers in America from physical persecution up to this point in time?

3. Describe other types of persecution that Christians in America may experience for their faith. Do you think these kinds of trials are comparable to physical suffering? Why or why not?

4. Relate an experience in your own life in which a particular trial was profitable. If you knew then what you know now, would you have chosen to endure that experience if you had been given a choice? Why or why not?

5. Do you think suffering tends to drive Christians closer to God or further away from God? What can a Christian do to make sure the former rather than the latter happens when he encounters trials?

6. What do you think is the most important thing individual Christians and churches should be doing to prepare for persecution?

7. Imagine you are in heaven having a conversation with a good friend, reminiscing about the most difficult situation you ever experienced while on earth. Do you think you will have a different feeling about that situation than you do now? Why?

## CHAPTER 7: Last-Days Living

1. Do you believe we are living in the last days? Should Christians be concerned with the answer to that question? Why or why not?

2. If you knew that you only had one year to live, what changes would you make in your life?

3. Why do you think Christians are reluctant to take courageous stands regarding their faith?

4. Do you believe there are any situations today in which Christians are justified in breaking the law? What are they? Would a Christian be justified in not paying his income tax, knowing that some of his money is being used to support abortions through Planned Parenthood? Why or why not?

5. Imagine you are standing before the judgment seat of Christ, as every believer will one day. What would God commend you for in your life? What do you imagine He would express disappointment over?

6. Up to this point, have you been living for the "dot" or for the "line"? What change could you make in your life right now that would make an eternal difference in your life and the lives of others?

7. What is the most important insight you have gained from this book?

NOTES

## CHAPTER 1: The Beginning of the End

1. Steve Holland, "Most Americans say U. S. on wrong track: Reuters/lpsos poll," Reuters, August 10, 2011, http://www.reuters.com/article/2011/08/11/us-usa-poll-idUSTRE7794EX20110811.

2. Associated Press, "Americans: My Faith Isn't the Only Way to Heaven," Fox News, June 24, 2008, http://www.foxnews.com/story/0,2933,370588,00.html.

3. Steve Blow, "Dallas pastor's broad-brush criticism of Islam goes way too far," *Dallas Morning News*, September 5, 2010, http://www.dallasnews.com/news/columnists/steve-blow/20100904-Dallas-pastor-s-broad-brush-criticism-8678.ece.

4. Ibid.

5. John Northcut, "Pastor of FBC Comments about Islam," September 11, 2010, comment on Robert Marus, "Baptist leaders meet with Holder, denounce Baptists trashing Islam," *Baptist Standard*, September 8, 2010, http://www.baptiststandard.com/index.php?option=com_content&task=view&id=11614&Itemid=53.

6. Robert Bork, *Slouching toward Gomorrah: Modern Liberalism and American Decline* (New York: Regan Books, 1996).

7. Joni Eareckson Tada, interview by Sarah Pulliam Bailey, "Joni Eareckson Tada on Something Greater than Healing," *Christianity Today*, October 8, 2010, http://www.christianitytoday.com/ct/2010/october/12.30.html?start=2.

8. Erwin W. Lutzer, *When a Nation Forgets God* (Chicago: Moody, 2010), 21–22.

9. A. W. Tozer, *The Knowledge of the Holy* (San Francisco: Harper and Row, 1961), 1.

10. Lutzer, *Nation Forgets God*, 89–90.

## CHAPTER 2: When a Nation Implodes

1. CNN Wire Staff, "Report: US-Canada Border Security Lacking," CNN, February 11, 2011, http://articles.cnn.com/2011-02-01/politics/u.s..canadian.border_1_border-security-northern-border-border-patrol-agents?_s=PM:POLITICS

2. John F. Frittelli, *Port and Maritime Security: Background and Issues* (New York: Novinka Books, 2003).

3. Paul Krugman, "The Dogbert theory of the debt," *New York Times,* November 30, 2009, http://krugman.blogs.nytimes.com/2009/11/30/the-dogbert-theory-of-the-debt/?scp=1&sq=%22George+Will%22%2B2019&st=nyt.

4. David Jeremiah, *The Coming Economic Armageddon* (New York: Faith Words, 2010), 7–9.

5. Engel, et al. v. Vitale, et al., 370 U.S. 421 (1962).

6. Robert Jeffress, *Outrageous Truth: Seven Absolutes You Can Still Believe* (Colorado Springs: WaterBrook, 2008), 174-178.

7. Lyle A. DeSpain and Mary R. DeSpain, et al. v. DeKalb County Community School District 428 et al., http://openjurist.org/384/f2d/836/lyle-a-despain-and-mary-r-despain-et-al-v-dekalbcounty-community-school-district-428-et-al.

8. Abington School District v. Schempp, 374 U.S. 203 (1963), quoted in Jeffress, *Outrageous Truth*, 224.

9. "Noteworthy Decisions Concerning Religion by the Supreme Court of the United States," Leadership U, updated July 14, 2002, http://www.leaderu.com/orgs/cdf/onug/decisions.html, quoted in Jeffress, *Outrageous Truth*, 223.

10. Stone v. Graham, 449 U.S. 39 (1980), quoted in Jeffress, *Outrageous Truth*, 225.

11. Robert Jeffress, "Air Force's pagan mistake," February 5, 2010, http://newsweek.washingtonpost.com/onfaith/guestvoices/2010/02/air_force_academys_pagan_mistake.html.

12. "Board enraged by any mention of 'God,'" WorldNetDaily, March 9, 2010, http://www.wnd.com/?pageId=127412.

13. Adam Lisberg, "Mayor Bloomberg Stands Up for Mosque," *New York Daily News,* August 3, 2010, http://www.nydailynews.com/blogs/dailypolitics/2010/08/bloomberg-stands-up-for-mosque.html.

14. Kelly Chernenkoff, "Hawaii Lawmakers Pass Bill to Create 'Islam Day,'" Fox News, May 6, 2009, http://www.foxnews.com/politics/2009/05/06/hawaii-lawmakers-pass-create-islam-day/.

15. "Can Christian Organizations Remain Christian in a 'Tolerant' Age?" Albert Mohler's website, March 22, 2010, http://www.albertmohler.com/2010/03/22/can-christian-organizations-remain-christian-in-a-tolerant-age/.

16. John Derbyshire, "George Washington Scofflaw University," National Review Online, October 27, 2010, http://www.nationalreview.com/blogs/print/251208.

17. Cathy Cleaver Ruse and William Saunders, Jr., *Partial Birth Abortion on Trial* (Washington D.C.: Family Research Council, 2006), 4–6.

18. Ibid., 3–4.

19. Ibid., 13.

20. Ibid., 16.

21. Barack Obama, address before Planned Parenthood Action Fund, July 2008, transcribed by Laura Echevarria, https://sites.google.com/site/lauraetch/barackobamabeforeplannedparenthoodaction.

22. "Obama Statement on 35th Anniversary of Roe v. Wade Decision," Reuters press release, January 22, 2008, http://www.reuters.com/article/2008/01/22/idUS218278+22-Jan-2008+BW20080122.

23. Ibid.

24. Dennis Howard, "The $35 Trillion Elephant in the Room" (The Movement for a Better America, 2008), quoted in Nelson Acquiliano, "Abortion Recession and the Economic Crisis," April 8, 2009, http://nelson-acquilano.suite101.com/abortion-recession-and-the-economic-crisis-a107429.

25. Laura Antikowiak, "What Do 40 Million Lost Lives Mean?" (National Right to Life, 2001), quoted in Nelson Acquiliano, "Abortion, Recession, and the Economic Crisis," Suite101, April 8, 2009, http://nelson-acquilano.suite101.com/abortion-recession-and-the-economic-crisis-a107429.

26. Lawrence v. Texas (02-102), 539 U.S. 558 (2003), Legal Information Institute, Cornell University Law School, http://www.law.cornell.edu/supct/html/02-102.ZO.html.

27. Dyana Bagby, "Gay, Bi Men 50 Times More Likely to Have HIV," (*Washington Blade*, August 28, 2009), quoted in "Homosexual, Bisexual Men 50 Times More Likely to Have HIV: CDC," Americans for Truth about Homosexuality, September 4, 2009, http://americansfortruth.com/2009/09/04/homosexual-bisexual-men-50-times-more-likely-to-have-hiv-cdc/.

28. Peter Sprigg, *The Top Ten Myths About Homosexuality* (Washington D.C.: Family Research Center, 2010), 26.

29. "State of the Movement Address by Matt Foreman, Executive Director, National Gay and Lesbian Task Force," press release, National Gay and Lesbian Task Force, February 8, 2008, http://www.thetaskforce.org/node/2710.

30. Sprigg, *Top Ten Myths*, 27.

31. Catherine M. Hutchinson et al., "Characteristics of Patients with Syphilis Attending Baltimore STD Clinics," *Archives of Internal Medicine* 151, no. 3 (1991): 511–516.

32. Sprigg, *Top Ten Myths*, 27.

33. Stephanie Wasserman, *HIV/AIDS facts to consider* (Denver: National Conference of State Legislatures, 1999), 37.

34. Lawrence v. Texas (02-102) 539 U.S. 558 (2003), Opinion [Kennedy], Legal Information Institute, Cornell University Law School, http://www.law.cornell.edu/supct/html/02-102.ZO.html.

35. Lawrence v. Texas (02-102) 539 U.S. 558 (2003), Dissent [Scalia], Legal Information Institute, Cornell University Law School, http://www.law.cornell.edu/supct/html/02-102.ZD.html.

36. *USA Today*, updated July 18, 2003, http://www.usatoday.com/news/washington/2003-07-17-court-usat_x.htm.

37. Frank Newport, "For First Time, Majority of Americans Favor Gay Marriage," Gallup, May 20, 2011, http://www.gallup.com/poll/147662/First-Time-Majority-Americans-Favor-Legal-Gay -Marriage.aspx.

38. Steven Waldman, "Abortion vs. Homosexuality: The Evangelical Age Gap," blog entry on Beliefnet.com, July 8, 2008, http://blog.beliefnet.com/stevenwaldman/2008/07/abortion-vs-homosexuality-the.html.

39. Event transcript, "A Post-Election Look at Religious Voters in the 2008 Election," The Pew Forum on Religion & Public Life, December 8, 2008, http://pewforum.org/Politics-and-Election-Look-at-Religious-Voters-in -the-2008-Election.aspx.

40. Staff editorial, "San Francisco should pursue gay marriage suit," Baylor University *Lariat*, February 27, 2004, quoted in "A Case Against Gay Marriage," *Christian Worldview Concepts*, March 2004, http://www.illinoisfamily.org/ACaseAgainstGayMarriage.pdf.

41. Kelley Beaucar Vlahos, "The Real Impact of Gay Marriage on Society," Fox News, March 22, 2004, http://www.foxnews.com/story/0,2933,114697,00.html.

42. Jennifer Marshall, *Marriage: What Social Science Says and Doesn't Say*, The Heritage Foundation, May 17, 2004, http://www.heritage.org/Research/Reports/2004/05/Marriage-What -Social-Science-Says-and-Doesnt-Say.

43. Sara McLanahan and Gary Sandefur, *Growing Up with a Single Parent: What Hurts, What Helps* (Cambridge, MA: Harvard University Press, 1994), 38.

44. David Popenoe, *Life without Father*, quoted in Charles Colson and Nancy Pearcey, "Why Not Gay Marriage?" *Christianity Today*, October 28, 1996, 104.

45. James Kent, *Commentaries on American Law, Vol. II*, (1838) in Charles J. Reid, Jr., "The Augustinian Goods of Marriage: The Disappearing Cornerstone of the American Law of Marriage," *The BYU Journal of Public Law* 18 (2004), quoted in Allan Carlson, "The Judicial Assault on the Family," *The Family in America* (April 2006), Howard Center for Family, Religion, and Society, http://www.profam.org/pub/fia/fia.2004.htm.

46. Allan Carlson, "The Judicial Assault on the Family," *The Family in America* (April 2006), Howard Center for Family, Religion, and Society, http://www.profam.org/pub/fia/fia.2004.htm.

47. Ibid.

## CHAPTER 3: The Most Misunderstood Word in America

1. "Gilbert K. Chesterton," Brainy Quote, June 17, 2011, http://www.brainyquote.com/quotes/quotes/g/gilbertkc163172.html.

2. Ayn Rand, *The Fountainhead* (New York: Penguin Books, 1952), 406.

3. Os Guinness, *Unspeakable: Facing Up to the Challenge of Evil* (New York: HarperCollins, 2005), 215.

4. Josh McDowell and Bob Hostetler, *The New Tolerance* (Wheaton, IL: Tyndale, 1998), 110.

5. Stephen Bates, "Religious Diversity and the Schools," *The American Enterprise* 4, no. 5 (September/October 1993), 18.

6. Lydia Saad, "Tolerance for Gay Rights at High Water Mark," Gallup News Service, May 29, 2007, http://www.gallup.com/poll/27694/tolerance-gay-rights-highwater-mark.aspx.

7. Randy Alcorn, *If God Is Good* (Colorado Springs, CO: Multnomah, 2009), 219.

8. "Americans Are Most Likely to Base Truth on Feelings," Barna Group, February 12, 2002, http://www.barna.org/barna-update/article/5-barna -update/67-americans-are-most-likely-to-base -truth-on-feelings.

9. Randy Alcorn, *Grace and Truth Paradox* (Sisters, OR: Multnomah, 2003), 41.

10. Norm Miller, "Fish Emphasizes Personal Evangelism," Baptist Press, June 19, 2007, http://www.baptistpress.com/printer -friendly.asp?ID=25929.

11. Ibid.

12. Gregory Kouki, "The Intolerance of Tolerance," Stand to Reason, http://www.str.org/site/News2?page=NewsArticle&id=5359.

13. *Webster's New World Dictionary,* Second College ed., s.v. "tolerance."

14. Kouki, "The Intolerance of Tolerance."

15. McDowell and Hostetler, *The New Tolerance,* 43.

16. Francis Schaeffer, *How Should We Then Live?* (Old Tappan, NJ: Fleming H. Revell, 1976), 145.

17. Pam Sheppard, "The Smithsonian/Sternberg Controversy: Cast doubt on Darwin, get cast out," Creation Ministries International, August 22, 2005, http://creation.com/the-smithsonian-sternberg-controversy.

18. Sarah Cassidy, "World scientists united to attack Creationism," *The Independent,* June 22, 2006, http://www.independent.co.uk/news/science/world -scientists-unite-to-attack-creationism-404985.html.

19. European Centre for Law and Justice, "Council of Europe passes resolution to ban creationism from classroom," press release, November 9, 2007, http://www.eclj.org/Releases/Read.aspx?GUID=fdf4728d-a1be-48ce-a0a9 -2f57715ef621&s=coe.

20. Alliance Defense Fund, "No choice: Doctors forced to perform abortions or else?", press release, http://www.alliancealert.org/2009/01/22/no-choice -doctors-forced-to-perform-abortions-or-else/.

21. Albert Mohler, "When Tolerance Doesn't Mean Toleration," *Albert Mohler* (blog), http://www.albertmohler.com/2006/09/07/when-tolerance-doesnt -mean-toleration/.

22. Charles G. Finney, "Lecture IV: Reproof, a Christian Duty," in *Lectures to*

*Professing Christians*, (New York, John S. Taylor, Brick Church Chapel, 1837), 47-48.

23. Joseph Story, *Commentaries on the Constitution of the United States* (Boston, MA: Hilliard, Gray, 1833), quoted in Dave Miller, "Islam and Early America," Apologetics Press, 2005, http://www.apologeticspress.org/apcontent. aspx?category=7&article=1485.

24. People v. Ruggles, "Amendment I (Religion)" Document 62, The Founders' Constitution, http://press-pubs.uchicago.edu/founders/documents/amendI_ religions62.html.

25. Henry P. Johnston, ed., *The Correspondence and Public Papers of John Jay* (New York: Burt Franklin, 1970) 4:393.

26. William Watkins, *The New Absolutes: How They Are Being Imposed On Us— How They Are Eroding Our Moral Landscape* (Minneapolis: Bethany House, 1996), 240.

## CHAPTER 4: How a Christian Should Vote

1. Francis Schaeffer, *Christian Manifesto* (Wheaton, IL: Crossway, 1981), 124.

2. Johnston, *John Jay*, 4:393.

3. Abraham Lincoln, "The Gettysburg Address," November 19, 1863, quoted in *The Collected Works of Abraham Lincoln*, ed. Roy P. Basler (New Brunswick, NJ: Rutgers UP, 1955).

4. Johnston, *John Jay*, 4:393.

5. Noah Webster, *Letters to a Young Gentleman Commencing His Education* (New Haven, S. Converse, 1823), 18–19.

6. John Witherspoon, "A Sermon Delivered at a Public Thanksgiving after Peace," *The Works of the Rev. John Witherspoon* (Edinburgh: J. Ogle, 1815) 4:266–267.

7. Robert Jeffress address to Religious Newswriters Annual Conference, Washington, D.C., September 19, 2008.

8. Julia Duin, "Secular Scribes Stunned," *Washington Times*, October 2, 2008.

9. Stephanie Cutter, "Vatican Cardinal Fuels Religious Dispute," CNN, April 23, 2004, http://articles.cnn.com/2004-04-23/world/vatican.kerry_1_ catholic-politicians-church-and-state-abortion-rights?_s=PM:WORLD.

10. George W. Bush, interview by Larry King, *Larry King Live*, August 12, 2004.

11. Barack Obama, interview by Sarah Pulliam and Ted Olsen, *Christianity Today,* January 23, 2008, http://www.christianitytoday.com/CT/2008/ januaryweb-only/104-32.0.html?start=2.

12. Barack Obama, Call to Renewal Keynote Address (Call to Renewal conference, Washington D.C., June 28, 2006), in Steven Waldman, "Obama's

Historic 'Call to Renewal' Speech," *Steven Waldman* (blog), Beliefnet.com, November 2, 2008, http://blog.beliefnet.com/stevenwaldman/2008/11/obamas-historic-call-to-renewa.html.

13. Barack Obama, *The Audacity of Hope* (Vintage Books, 2006), 108.

14. Art Moore, "Court strikes down Texas sodomy law," June 26,2003, World Net Daily, http://www.wnd.com/?pageId=19490.

15. Rust v. Sullivan (89-1391, 92) 500 U.S. 173 (1991), Dissent [Blackman], Legal Information Institute, Cornell University Law School, http://www.law.cornell.edu/supct/html/historics/USSC_CR_0500_10173_ZD.html.

16. 2008 Official Presidential General Election Results, http://www.fec.gov/pubrec/fe2008/2008presgeresults.pdf.

17. John Jay, *The Correspondence and Public Papers of John Jay* (New York: Putnam and Sons, 1890), 161.

18. Dr. Jeff Myers, "Politics: Should Christians Get Involved?" Christianity, http://www.christianity.com/1128040/.

19. Chuck Colson, "Should Christians Go Into Politics?" Colson Center, August 24,2009, http://www.colsoncenter.org/the-center/columns/colson-files/12305-should-christians-go-into-politics.

## CHAPTER 5: For Pastors Only

1. Dwight Edwards, *Releasing the Rivers Within* (Colorado Springs: Water-Brook, 2003), 45.

2. Douglas LeBlanc, "Wildheart," *Christianity Today,* August 2004, http://www.christianitytoday.com/ct/2004/august/14.30.html?start=1.

3. Michael Horton, *Christless Christianity* (Grand Rapids: Baker, 2008), 203.

4. "New Study Identifies the Strongest and Weakest Character Traits of Christian Leaders," Barna Group, January 13, 2003, http://www.barna.org/barna-update/article/5-barnaupdate/113-new-study-identifies-the-strongest-and-weakestcharacter-traits-of-christian-leaders?q=generational+differences.

5. Horton, *Christless Christianity*, 203.

6. John Ortberg, *Everybody's Normal Till You Get to Know Them* (Grand Rapids: Zondervan, 2003), 221.

7. Larry Dixon, "The Doctrine of the Church", *Emmaus Journal* 13 (Winter 2004): http://www.galaxie.com/article/7833.

8. Nelson Mandela, in Gordon MacDonald, *A Resilient Life* (Nashville: Thomas Nelson, 2004), 219-20.

9. Eugene Peterson, in Philip Yancey, *Reaching for the Invisible God* (Grand Rapids: Zondervan, 2000), 155.

10. John Maxwell, *The Twenty-One Irrefutable Laws of Leadership* (Nashville: Thomas Nelson, 1998), 1.

11. Adrian Rogers, in Brett Champion, "Living without Spirit's power is a sin, Adrian Rogers says," Baptist Press, posted October 13, 1999, http://www.bpnews.net/bpnews.asp?id=88.

12. Eugene Peterson, *Working the Angles* (Grand Rapids, MI: William Eerdmans, 1987), 1–2.

13. Charles Spurgeon, in Stephen J. Lawson, "The Reformation of the Pulpit" (unpublished manuscript, 2006), New Reformation website, posted September 5, 2007, http://www.newreformationministries.org/home/140001931/140001931/files/The%20Reformation%20of%20the%20Pulpit.pdf.

14. Steven J. Lawson, *Famine in the Land* (Chicago: Moody, 2003), 98.

15. Stephen F. Olford, *Anointed Expository Preaching* (Nashville: Broadman & Holman, 1998), 69.

16. Lawson, *Famine in the Land*, 66.

17. John Ortberg, *The Life You've Always Wanted* (Grand Rapids: Zondervan, 1997), 188.

18. Olford, *Anointed Expository Preaching*, 68.

19. George Stibitz, "The Old Testament Prophets As Social Reformers," in *The Biblical World*, ed. William R. Harper, vol. 12, 1898 (Chicago: University of Chicago Press, 1898), 22–23.

20. Johnston, *John Jay*, 4:393.

21. Erik Stanley, "Pulpit Initiative about Freedom, not Politics," *Washington Post*, September 25, 2008, http://newsweek.washingtonpost.com/onfaith/guestvoices/2008/09/pulpit_initiative_about_freedo.html.

22. Michael Willhoite, *Daddy's Roommate* (Los Angeles, Alyson Publications, 1990); Lesléa Newman, *Heather Has Two Mommies* (Los Angeles, Alyson Publications, 1989).

23. Willhoite, *Daddy's Roommate*, 16.

24. Lawson, *Famine in the Land*, 67.

25. Bill Hybels, "From the Beginning, Part 4: Become Fully Devoted Followers" (Willow Creek Community Church, 2000): http://www.willowcreek.com/wca_prodsb.asp?invtid=PR03884.

26. Jim Cymbala, *Fresh Wind, Fresh Fire* (Grand Rapids: Zondervan, 1997), 125–126.

## CHAPTER 6: When Persecution Comes

1. Tim Stafford, "The Pastor Without a Paycheck," *Christianity Today*, April 2003, http://www.christianitytoday.com/ct/2003/april/7.90.html?start=1.

2. Ibid.

3. Chuck Colson, "A New Century of Martyrs", BreakPoint, June 14, 2002, http://www.breakpoint.org/commentaries/3076-a-new-century-of-martyrs.

4. "Young Americans still lack basic global knowledge, National Geographic-Roper survey shows," *National Geographic*, press release, May 2, 2006, http://press.nationalgeographic.com/pressroom/index.jsp?siteID=1&pageID=pressReleases_detail&cid=1146580209503.

5. "Iraq: Three Christians Killed," *Voice of the Martyrs*, April 27, 2009, http://www.persecution.com/public/newsroom.aspx?story_ID=MTEz.

6. Brian Murphy, Associated Press, "Iran rounds up Christians in crackdown," ABC News, January 11, 2011, http://abcnews.go.com/International/wireStory?id=12590821.

7. "Afghanistan: Christian Imprisoned," *Voice of the Martyrs*, last updated January 7, 2011, http://www.persecution.com/public/newsroom.aspx?story_ID=MzI5.

8. Associated Press, "Egypt Church Bomb Kills 21 at New Year's Mass," CBS News, January 1, 2011, http://www.cbsnews.com/stories/2010/12/31/world/main7201972.shtml.

9. "China", Voice of the Martyrs, 2011, http://www.persecution.net/china.htm.

10. Philip Yancey, *What Good Is God?* (New York: Faith Words, 2010), 49-50.

11. Ibid., 51.

12. David Jeremiah, *The Coming Economic Armageddon* (New York: Faith Words, 2010), 131,148- 49

13. Jeremiah, *Economic Armageddon*, 133.

14. John Adams, quoted in Jeffress, *Outrageous Truth*, 173.

15. "Tacitus (c. 55–117 CE): Nero's persecution of the Christians," Washington State University website, http://public.wsu.edu/~wldciv/world_civ_reader/world_civ_reader_1/tacitus.html.

16. Frank Payne, "My Worst Year in Ministry," *Christianity Today*, April 1, 2002, http://www.christianitytoday.com/le/2002/spring/15.106.html.

17. Charles R. Swindoll, *Job* (Nashville: Thomas Nelson, 2004), 217.

18. Dallas Willard, *The Spirit of the Disciplines* (San Francisco: Harper and Row, 1988), 35.

19. David Jeremiah, *Searching for Heaven on Earth* (Nashville: Thomas Nelson, 2004), 74–75.

20. Lee Strobel, *The Case for Faith* (Grand Rapids: Zondervan, 2000), 47.

21. Dan Wooding, "Trojan Horse of Success," quoted in Stu Weber, *Spirit Warriors: Strategies for the Battles Christian Men and Women Face Every Day* (Multnomah, 2003), 44.

## CHAPTER 7: Last-Days Living

1. Dennis McKinsey, ed., "Imminence" in *Biblical Errancy*, issue 89 (May 1990).

2. David Jeremiah, *Living with Confidence in a Chaotic World* (Nashville: Thomas Nelson, 2009), 188.

3. Philip Caulfield, "Terror Threat in U.S. is highest since 9/11, Homeland Security Secretary Napolitano says," *NY Daily News*, February 9, 2011, http://articles.nydailynews.com/2011-02-09/news/28550750_1_terror -threat-terrorist-threat-american-born-cleric.

4. Eugene H. Peterson, *A Long Obedience in the Same Direction* (Downers Grove, IL: InterVarsity, 1980), 52.

5. Lee Strobel, *The Case for Faith* (Grand Rapids: Zondervan, 2000), 217.

6. G. Campbell Morgan, quoted in Jeremiah, *Chaotic World*, 135.

7. Martin Luther King Jr., "Letter from a Birmingham Jail," April 16, 1963, University of Pennsylvania African Studies Center, http://www.africa.upenn .edu/Articles_Gen/Letter_Birmingham.html

8. Eddie Barker, ed., "Book Bans: Who Has Right to Decide What Other People Read?" *Wichita Falls Times Record News*, June 16, 1998, 6B.

9. Author unknown.

10. Ben Patterson, "Have I Become Useless?" *Leadership Journal*, Summer 2004, http://www.christianitytoday.com/le/2004/summer/12.68.html?start=1.

11. Randy Alcorn, *The Treasure Principle* (Sisters, OR: Multnomah, 2001), 48–49.

12. Andrew J. Horner, *By Chance or By Design?* (Dallas: Premier Designs, 2010), 79.

# ABOUT THE AUTHOR

**Robert Jeffress** (DMin, Southwestern Theological Seminary; ThM, Dallas Theological Seminary) is an author and the senior pastor of the 10,000-member First Baptist Church of Dallas, Texas. His bold, biblical, and practical approach to ministry has made him one of the country's most respected evangelical leaders and earned him a Daniel Award from Vision America. He regularly appears on major mainstream media outlets such as Fox News, CNN, MSNBC, *The O'Reilly Factor, Cavuto on Business*, ABC's *Good Morning America*, and CBS's *The Early Show*. He also hosts a television program, *Pathway to Victory*, and teaches a daily sermon series that airs on 1,200 television stations and cable systems throughout the nation and in 28 countries around the world.

## WORTHY
### PUBLISHING

## IF YOU LIKED THIS BOOK . . .

- Tell your friends by going to: www.twilightslastgleaming.net and clicking "LIKE"

- Share the video book trailer by posting it on your Facebook page

- Head over to our Facebook page, click "LIKE" and post a comment regarding what you enjoyed about the book

- Tweet "I recommend reading #Twilight'sLastGleaming by @robertjeffress @Worthypub"

- Hashtag: #Twilight'sLastGleaming

- Subscribe to our newsletter by going to http://worthypublishing.com/about/subscribe.php

**WORTHY PUBLISHING
FACEBOOK PAGE**

**WORTHY PUBLISHING
WEBSITE**